DEAR ERNEST AND JULIO...

DEAR ERNEST AND JULIO...

The Ordinary Guy's Search for the Extraordinary Job

BY FRED GRIMES

WITH DAVID FREED

ST. MARTIN'S GRIFFIN
NEW YORK

Design by Diane Stevenson of SNAP-HAUS Graphics

Library of Congress Cataloging-in-Publication Data

Grimes, Fred,
    Dear Ernest and Julio: the ordinary guy's search for the
extraordinary job / Fred Grimes.
        p.   cm.
    ISBN 0–312–15511–5
    1. Job hunting—Humor   I. Title
    HF5382.7.G736   1997
    650.14'02'07—dc21   97–6379

First St. Martin's Griffin Edition: June 1997

10 9 8 7 6 5 4 3 2 1

FOR
THE WIFE
AND KIDS

ACKNOWLEDGMENTS

First of all I would like to thank my friend Dave for letting me use his computer so I could write the million or so letters I have written and continue to write in my search for a great job.

I want to thank the teachers at Dennis Franklin Community College for teaching me how to be a good writer.

I owe a big thanks to my Boss for downsizing the plant which caused me to lose my job to begin with which caused me to start thinking about getting a better job which caused me to send out all the letters which this book is about.

I would like to thank the many nice people who wrote me back and then said it was okay to put their letters in the book. Even though they did not give me a job I still think they are great for at least taking the time. Not everybody was so willing to help out, I am here to tell you.

Take Charlton Heston. A great actor. Who could forget *Planet of the Apes*? I wrote him saying he should run for president and I would be his campaign manager. He wrote back saying it is more fun playing a politician in the movies than being one in real life. I asked if it was okay to put his letter in my book. His publicist said forget it.

Ditto the Power Rangers. I told them I thought they needed new blood—a slower, nonviolent Ranger "Dad." A Ranger Dad who talks his way out of trouble instead of kicking and karate chopping his way out. I volunteered for the job. They turned me down and said they didn't want their letter in any book.

Then there was Macy's department store. They rejected my idea that they hire me to be a full-time Santa. Said they wanted to "keep the process of selecting Santa's helpers as discreet as possible."

Whatever that means.

Anyway, thanks to Doug Barr, Mitch Bates, Karoline Biggs, Steve Delsohn, Dave Fox, Scott Harris, Hoyt Hillsman, E. L. Pavelka, Phil Reed, Shari Wenk, Steve Wick, Tim Wurtz, and all the other good folks down at the plant who have helped me to hang in there in my search for a good job.

And last but not least, I want to thank you for at least thinking about buying my book which for the price I think is a pretty good deal.

INTRODUCTION

Used to be in this Great Country of ours, a guy would get a job, work his way up, raise The Kids, pay off the house, then buy himself a Winnebago, go fishing whenever he wanted, and watch *I Dream of Jeannie* reruns the rest of his life. The American Dream.

I had a job like that. Down at the plant. Then one day I did not have a job. The Boss said he was sorry. Said it had to do with something he called "corporate downsizing." To which I said, "Hey, Boss, downsize this." Pardon my French. Anyway, the point is, I found myself unemployed for the first time in my life. With a lot of time to think about things.

I remembered what my Dad used to tell me. We'd be out on the lake, going after wily Mr. Bass. "Fred," Dad would say, a night crawler squiggling between his fingers, "this is America. Land of Opportunity. You can be anything. Do anything. You just got to try."

Try.

From the day we are born in this country we grow up dreaming about being an astronaut or a ball player, working at *Playboy* magazine or being ambassador to Hawaii. Whatever. Truth is, most of us end up down at the plant, putting in five days a week, fifty weeks a year, just to pay the bills. After a while, we just stop trying.

After I lost my job, The Wife says to me, "Fred, get yourself out of that recliner and go get a regular job with a regular paycheck because The Kids need new socks and the only food we have in the house is instant Cream of Wheat." To which I replied, "What would it say to The Kids if I got me just another job at another plant?" This is America. Land of Opportunity! No sir, I want a great job. The job of my dreams. I am going to try.

As you will see, I have been trying for a while now. It has been no picnic, let me tell you. I have sent out about a million applications so far and the nearest I have come to getting hired is by the Navy. I wanted to be a frogman. I think they wanted me to mop decks. Some people might have given up by now. Like my cousin Berf. "When the going gets tough," Berf likes to say, "the tough go down to Jumbo's Clown Room and have a shot or two." I remember in third grade when Berf wanted to be president. These days he works housewares over at Wal-Mart. Not that working housewares at Wal-Mart is bad. It is just not for me. And I bet not for you.

If you go to sleep at night with a dream of doing something more, something big, just do it. Aim high. Go for the gusto. This is America. You can be whatever you want. All you got to do is try.

And if you hear of any great jobs, lemme know.

Fred Grimes

FRED GRIMES

4087 San Rafael Avenue
Los Angeles, CA 90065

July 14, 1995

Newt Gingrich, Speaker of the House
Rayburn House Office Building
Washington, D.C. 20515

Dear Mr. Speaker:

I understand we (U.S.) have a "poet laureat." Do you know anything about this, sir? If so, I sure would appreciate you putting me in for the job as I could really use it.

Before I lost my job down at the plant I would make up poems in my head just to try and block out all the noise and keep my mind active. No one told me you could make money from them. You probably won't believe this, but I consider myself a patroit and a lot of the ones I made up are patriotic. Here is one of my favorites.

Here's a story
About a flag named Glory
With 13 stripes and many little stars.
I get to crying
When it is flying
Because there is so much his-to-ry.

I do not want to brag but my wife and my friend Dave (who went to college and is letting me borrow his computer to write this) both say I am a poet "who don't know it." (get it?)

Mr. Gingrich, is the job filled? I hope not. Thank you for your prompt attention to this matter.

Sincerely,

Fred Grimes

Fred Grimes

FRED GRIMES

4087 San Rafael Avenue
Los Angeles, CA 90065

July 26, 1995

Mr. Warren Christopher, secretary of state
2201 E. St. N.W.
Washington, D.C. 20520

Dear Mr. Secretary:

I would like to be an ambassador and am hoping you can help me.

Let me be right up front sir. I have never been a diplomat. I realize my chances of getting to be ambassador to somewhere like England or Cancun are slim. But what about all those other places that have shall we say, less than universal appeal? (I will not mention them by name, but I think you know which ones I am talking about). My plan sir is to start out in one of these places pay my dues and work my way up. Consider that I am:

* Typical, loyal American with typical American sensibilities.
* Presently unemployed and willing to relocate.
* No felony convictions.
* References on request.

Mr. Secretary I am ready willing and able to represent my country. You just tell me where to go, and I am there! Just out of curiosity how much would the job pay and would it come with gardener, house boy etc.?

Please let me know ASAP as I am presently exploring many other employment possibilities and anticipate several offers in the immediate future.

Respectfully submitted,

Fred Grimes

Fred Grimes

P.S.--Please <u>do not</u> consider me for any ambassadorhoods in France.

United States Department of State

Washington, D.C.   20520

Thank you for your recent inquiry concerning the Foreign Service Officer Examination.

- The U.S Department of State has decided not to offer the exam in 1995.

- The decision was made because of government downsizing and the adequate supply of highly qualified applicants already in the pipeline to fill the expected number of vacancies.

- The next exam will be in fall of 1996.

Registration forms for the 1996 exam will be available <u>after May 1996</u> by writing:

Recruitment Division - FSWE
The Department of State
P.O. Box 12226
Arlington, Virginia 22219

-The Recruitment Division

FRED GRIMES

4087 San Rafael Avenue
Los Angeles, CA 90065

July 26, 1995

David Wilhelm, chairman
Democratic National Committee
430 S. Capitol St. S.E.
Washington, D.C. 20003

Dear Mr. Wilhelm:

Every time you Democrats have a convention you bring in some big singer to sing the National Anthem to open things up. Well I would like to put in the for the job.

I am the first to admit that I cannot sing to save my life. The wife reminds me of this every morning when I am in the shower. But I think this makes me the perfect candidate for the job. Sir think about it. An average unemployed American (me) gets up and sings the National Anthem in front of the entire Country. Hollywood makes a movie about it. I finally find a job. And millions of other unemployed Americans get inspired. How many votes do you think you would get? Millions!

I would be willing to register Democrat and maybe even vote Democrat if you offer me the job.

One thing I should tell you up front is that I have made this exact same offer to the "other party" (GOP) and am waiting on them to get back to me.

Please do not let this golden opportunity pass you up.

Sincerely,

Fred Grimes
Fred Grimes

P.S.--References on request.

CHICAGO

DEBRA DELEE, CEO

October 24 , 1995

Mr. Fred Grimes
4087 San Rafael Avenue
Los Angeles, CA 90065

Dear Mr. Grimes:

Thank you again for your interest in the Democratic National Convention! The dates of the Convention are Monday, August 26, 1996 through Thursday, August 29, 1996, and it will be held at the new United Center.

As you can imagine, a convention of this size involves many different facets and different start dates, and many individuals have already expressed an interest in working for the Convention. Therefore, at this time, we want to provide you with a clearer understanding of the different positions available and our estimated time frame.

The Convention is being planned in four (4) main phases:

- **Phase I: September - December, 1995** -- mainly logistical and operational departments (administration, housing, technology, transportation).
- **Phase II: January - April, 1996** -- all communication, press and media operations, with start-up operations for all departments.
- **Phase III: April - June, 1996** -- all departments operating, with heavy concentration on Communications and Hall activities.
- **Phase IV: July - August, 1996** -- all departments of the Convention in fast gear, with primary emphasis on credentials and production.

Enclosed you will find a brief description of the many different Convention departments and the estimated time for hiring by those departments. We have also attached a brief Employment Questionnaire, designed to help you better choose the area most suited to your experience.

Once we have received your completed Questionnaire, we plan to submit these to the Deputy CEOs or to the Division Directors for their review. Most departments will have at minimum a Director (pay scale: $40,000-70,000), Deputy/Executive ($25,000-40,000) and an Assistant ($15,000-25,000). You will see on the Questionnaire that you will <u>not</u> be considered for jobs which pay less than you indicate. And unfortunately, no housing or moving costs can be paid for people moving to Chicago to work on the Convention.

Please return the completed Questionnaire (along with a copy of your resume and list of references) to: Democratic National Convention, P.O. Box 641196, Chicago, Illinois 60664-1196, Attention: Employment Questionnaire. **Sorry, but no phone calls or faxes please**.

Thanks again for your interest and we look forward to a great 1996 Convention!

Sincerely,

Bradley J. Kiley

Bradley J. Kiley
Director of Administration

DEMOCRATIC NATIONAL CONVENTION
P.O. BOX 641196 • CHICAGO, IL 60664-1196 • TEL (312) 832-1996 • FAX (312) 832-2515

5

RESUME OF FRED GRIMES

Fred Grimes
4087 San Rafael Avenue
Los Angeles, California 90065

OBJECTIVE

A great job

PERSONAL HISTORY

Married. Wife and kids.

EDUCATION

Graduate Of High School
Community College (one quarter)

EMPLOYMENT HISTORY

Worked down at plant before losing job.

SPECIAL INTERESTS

Fishing, archery, bowling, t.v., eating.

REFERENCES

on request.

DEMOCRATIC NATIONAL CONVENTION
EMPLOYMENT QUESTIONNAIRE

Please type or print.

GENERAL INFORMATION

FRED GRIMES
1. Name (Last, First, Middle)

4087 SAN RAFAEL AVENUE   LOS ANGELES
2. Mailing Address   3. City   4. State/Zip Code
CALIFORNIA 90065

( ) CANNOT AFFORD ( ) UNEMPLOYED
5. Home Phone   6. Work Phone

$ 70,000 00

7. What is the lowest annual pay you will accept? You will **not** be considered for jobs which pay less than you indicate. Most departments have a Director ($40-70,000); a Deputy/Executive ($25-40,000); and an Assistant ($15-25,000).

AREA OF INTEREST   SINGING NATIONAL ANTHEM

8. For those seeking both paid and volunteer positions, **please indicate in preference order from 1-5**, with 1 being your first choice, the departments you would like to be considered for.

DEPARTMENT	AREA OF INTEREST	DEPARTMENT	AREA OF INTEREST
Administration		Press	
Budget/Finance		Production	
Communications		Public Liaison	
Credentials		Satellite News	
General Counsel		Security	
Hall Construction		Technology	
Headquarter Hotel		Transportation	
Housing		**ANY OF THE ABOVE**	
Media Arrangements			

VOLUNTEERS

9. Please check here if you would like to be considered for the many volunteer opportunities available.

Although we may already have them on file, **PLEASE ATTACH A RESUME AND A LIST OF REFERENCES TO THIS FORM** and return to the Democratic National Convention, P.O. Box 641196, Chicago, Illinois 60664-1196, Attention: Employment Questionnaire Dept. Thank you.

CHICAGO

DEBRA DELEE, CEO

January 10, 1996

Mr. Fred Grimes
4087 San Rafael Avenue
Los Angeles, CA 90065

Dear Mr. Grimes:

Thank you for completing and returning your questionnaire for employment with the 1996 Democratic National Convention.

Your resume has been added to our database for review by the appropriate Convention division directors. These individual directors are responsible for the hiring of positions in the areas you specified. You may hear from one or more of these directors over the next few months should they be interested in your application. If you do not hear from us within the next few months other candidates may have been chosen.

Again, I'd like to thank you for your interest in working with the 1996 Democratic National Convention.

Sincerely,

Bradley J. Kiley
Director of Administration

FRED GRIMES

4087 San Rafael Avenue
Los Angeles, CA 90065

July 26, 1995

Mr. Philip N. Diehl, director
U.S. Mint
633 3rd St. N.W.
Washington, D.C. 20220

Dear Mr. Diehl:

I would like to make money.

How do I go about getting work at the mint? I do not have a preference as to what kind of money I make--the size I mean. Do you still make silver dollars? That might be nice.

I have never made money before (in more ways than one) but being a regular working man I have a lot of experience working with my hands (references on request). Until recently I worked down at the plant. Now I am unemployed.

I would be happy to talk to you about working whatever shift you may have available. The only question I have is what about the discarded money? When I was down at the plant we got to keep all the fixtures that come off the line a little bit ruined. Would I get to keep the money that has flaws in it? Just curious.

Well, that about wraps it up.

Sincerely,

Fred Grimes

Fred Grimes

P.S.--I could start immediately.

DEPARTMENT OF THE TREASURY
UNITED STATES MINT
WASHINGTON, D.C. 20220

August 9, 1995

Mr. Fred Grimes
4087 San Rafael Avenue
Los Angeles, California   90065

Dear Mr. Grimes:

Thank you for your entertaining letter. I certainly understand your interest in making money. Here at the United States Mint we have a special affinity for that endeavor.

With a thought to getting a better sense of what you had in mind, we did try to call you at home and were disappointed to find no telephone listing for you. As you might guess, we need a little more to go on regarding your qualifications and your specific goals.

My suggestion is that you contact the Personnel Officer in our San Francisco Mint or, if you wish to look at farther reaches, any of our other Mints. You will be able to find out from them when jobs might be available that match your skills and preferences. Their names, addresses, and telephone numbers are provided on the enclosed listing.

In the interim, you might enjoy reading some material about the United States Mint, which is also enclosed. If I can be of further assistance to you, please let me know. I wish you success in your quest to make money.

Sincerely,

Larry A. Brock
Assistant Director for
    Human Resources

Enclosures

9

FRED GRIMES

4087 San Rafael Avenue
Los Angeles, CA 90065

July 26, 1995

Mr. Bill Clinton, U.S.A President
The White House
1600 Pennsylvania Avenue N.W.
Washington, D.C. 20500

Dear Mr. President:

I know that this economy thing is real big with you. Sometimes I wonder if you realize
how big it is among us "little" folks. Take me for example. I lost my job down at the plant.
Now I am looking for work.

You and me have many things in common, Mr. President. One thing is cats. We both have
one. My cat is named Roy. I have seen your cat Socks on t.v. I know a Secret Service
agent guards him. Why? Mr. President, let us be honest. Do we (U.S. taxpayers) really
need a Secret Service agent guarding your cat?

I would like to apply for the job. I am good with cats (references on request). Socks
seems like a nice cat. A lot nicer than Roy. I would take better care of Socks than some
agent and at probably a lot less cost! In this age of deficits every penny counts, right?

Sir, I voted for you. Maybe you can return the favor and put me back to work.

Respectfully,

Fred Grimes

Fred Grimes

P.S.--You would have my support in 1996!

THE WHITE HOUSE

WASHINGTON

August 28, 1995

Mr. Fred Grimes
4087 San Rafael Avenue
Los Angeles, California 90065

Dear Mr. Grimes:

Thank you for your kind offer.

Although the President is unable to accept your services,
on his behalf I want to extend gratitude for the spirit of
generosity and cooperation that prompted your offer.

President Clinton appreciates your support.

Sincerely,

James A. Dorskind
Special Assistant to the President
Director of Correspondence and
Presidential Messages

FRED GRIMES

4087 San Rafael Avenue
Los Angeles, CA 90065

July 26, 1995

Tommy Lasorda, manager
Los Angeles Dodgers
P.O. Box 51100
Los Angeles, CA 90074-1100

Dear Tommy:

Do you have any openings for a bullpen catcher, base coach, warm-up pitcher or radar gun operator? If so I would to apply for the job.

My dad used to tell me, Fred, when life throws you a curve, wait for the cheese. That is what I am doing. You see Tommy, (I hope you do not mind me calling you Tommy. I feel like I know you so well having seen you so often at Dodger Stadium and on those weight loss commercials), I am unemployed. But being without work has opened my eyes to many new occupational possibilities. Like baseball.

My friend Dave and I were at the stadium last month. Watching you pitch batting practice, the thought hit me like a fast ball: I could do that and how much does it pay?

I am not bragging Tommy, but when I played for the plant softball team (references on request), they called me Freddie Hustle. So I do know a little bit about the game. I am no spring chicken anymore. I could never actually play for the Dodgers. But I believe I can still be a productive member of the best darned baseball team on earth!

Talk about public relations. You hire me, an average fan, to pitch warm-up. My success story would inspire million of fans who are still mad over the strike to start going to Dodger Stadium and spend like crazy. Tommy, remember "Field of Dreams?"--if you hire me, they will come.

Go Dodgers,

Fred Grimes

Fred Grimes

LOS ANGELES Dodgers®

IRENE H. TANJI
DIRECTOR, HUMAN RESOURCES
AND ADMINISTRATION
(213) 224-1547

1000 ELYSIAN PARK AVENUE
LOS ANGELES, CA 90012-1199

August 1, 1995

Fred Grimes
4087 San Rafael Avenue
Los Angeles, CA 90065

Dear Mr. Grimes:

    Thank you for your letter of July 26, 1995 and for your interest in the Dodgers. At this time, we do not have any bullpen catcher positions available. However, please check with us again in the future regarding any employment opportunities that may develop with the company.

    Again, thank you for your interest in the Dodgers, and best wishes for success in all future endeavors.

Sincerely,

Irene H. Tanji
Director, Human Resources and
Administration

IHT/jl

FRED GRIMES

4087 San Rafael Avenue
Los Angeles, CA 90065

July 26, 1995

Mr. Mike Espy, secretary of agriculture
14th St. and Independence Ave.
Washington, D.C. 20250

Dear. Mr. Secretary Espy:

I was out in the yard today digging out dandelions when I had a thought that I believe could change my life forever. Please allow me to explain.

I am presently unemployed. Lost my job down at the plant. Because I have a lot of time on my hands, my yard is looking <u>real</u> good, I am happy to say. Anyway I had this thought: if I can take care of a lawn, why not try farming? Granted, I live in the middle of a city and have never set foot on a farm, but being an American all about "can do" rather than "cannot", right?

Mr. Espy for your information my backyard is approx. 40x50'. What crops might grow best back there in this climate etc.? Better yet what crops might grow "too" well, if you get my drift. In other words sir, what crops would the government pay me <u>not</u> to grow? I am not trying to rip anybody off, but if you folks are willing to pay big farmers not to grow zucchinis or whatever, why can't we people in the city take advantage of the same opportunity?

I know the fall planting season is still a few months off yet, but I thought I better write now so as to get ready. Please advise.

Sincerely yours,

Fred Grimes

Fred Grimes

United States
Department of
Agriculture

Consolidated
Farm Service
Agency

P.O. Box 2415
Washington, D.C.
20013-2415

AUG 1 5 1995

Mr. Fred Grimes
4087 San Rafael Avenue
Los Angeles, California 90065

Dear Mr. Grimes:

Thank you for your request to former Secretary of Agriculture Mike Espy for information on how one may receive a Federal subsidy for not raising crops. Because of the topic of your letter, Secretary Glickman has asked me to respond on his behalf.

Under current programs for wheat, feed grains, cotton and rice, persons "actively engaged in farming" receive several types of benefits, including price support for production of these crops and deficiency payments. Depending on current and expected stock levels, program participants may be required to reduce their planted acreage of these crops in order to be eligible for these price and income supports.

The Food Security Act of 1985, as amended, authorizes the Conservation Reserve Program which allows producers of crops to bid for annual rental payments they will accept from the Commodity Credit Corporation in return for retiring highly erodible and other environmentally sensitive cropland for 10 years. The program is intended to reduce soil erosion on enrolled acreage and reduce sedimentation in streams and lakes.

While participating in Department of Agriculture price support programs with a 40 foot by 50 foot "farm" is not practical, you can obtain more information from the Los Angeles County Consolidated Farm Service Agency Office. The telephone number there is (805) 942-9549.

Thank you again for your letter.

Sincerely,

JAMES A. LANGLEY

for Larry Walker

FRED GRIMES

4087 San Rafael Avenue
Los Angeles, CA 90065

July 28, 1995

Penny Masters, director of human resources
SeaWorld
1720 South Shores Road
San Diego, California 92109

Dear Ms. Masters:

Before I lost my job the wife and I took our kids to see Shamu. It cost us more than $100 to get in but it was worth every penny. That whale is <u>smart</u>. We loved it when he waved his tail. And those trainers looked like they were having a ball. Which is why I am writing you.

Ms. Masters I would like to be a whale trainer.

I do not have any experience with whales or anything like that. But before you throw out my letter let me just say this. If you can train a stubborn dumb cat to stop scratching at your door at 3 in the morning (which I have done successfully, references on request), how hard can it be to teach an intelligent fish to splash a bunch of tourists on command?

I believe I have a way with animals. I would like to show you. Maybe I can come down there one day with the family. As I am presently unemployed and looking for a job my schedule is wide open. If you could see fit to give us free pass, the family could wander around while I put Shamu through his paces. I just know we would get along.

I am looking forward to hearing from you.

Sincerely,

Fred Grimes

Fred Grimes

*Thank you for applying
for a position at Sea World.*

*At this time we do not have a suitable
position available for you. For current
openings, Please stay in contact
with our Job Line by calling
(619) 226-3861.*

*Again, thank you for your interest.
Good luck in your job search.*

Sea World.

FRED GRIMES

4087 San Rafael Avenue
Los Angeles, CA 90065

August 4, 1995

Penny Masters, director of human resources
SeaWorld
1720 South Shores Road
San Diego, California 92109

Dear Ms. Masters

Well I called the Job Line per the note you sent. It said you are looking for food services line cook with experience in food prep, broiler work or sawtay.

Ms. Masters maybe you did not read my letter close enough but I want to be a whale trainer not a cook.

As I mentioned I have a way with animals and I think Shamu and I would get along fine.

Sincerely,

Fred Grimes

Fred Grimes

P.S.--I am not looking for a free pass or nothing. I am looking for a good job!

Sea World
of California

Sea World of San Diego
Employment Center

We thank you for submitting a resume for an animal trainer in Sea
World of San Diego's animal training department.

Although we were impressed by your resume, we have found other
candidates who more closely suit our needs at this time. For
current openings, please stay in contact with our Job Line by
calling (619) 226-3861.

Again, thank you for your interest. Good luck in your job search.

Sincerely,

Jeff Langston
Supervisor
Employment Center

Sea World of California
1720 South Shores Road
San Diego, CA 92109-7995
(619) 222-6363

**Busch Entertainment
Corporation**
ONE OF THE ANHEUSER BUSCH COMPANIES

FRED GRIMES

4087 San Rafael Avenue
Los Angeles, CA 90065

July 26, 1995

Deb Stevens, personnel manager
Cunard Cruise Ship Lines
555 5th St.
New York, N.Y. 10017

Dear Ms. Stevens:

Recently I went fishing with my friend Dave in his new boat. He let me have a turn at the wheel and except for the getting ill part I did fine. Which made me think of something. How can I become a steamship captain?

I have never been on a cruise. Also I tend to get a little sea sick which Dave says you get used to. I realize that with no experience I would be the last person on earth you would want driving one of those big passenger ships! But I am a quick learner (references on request). With a few weeks training taking it slow I bet I could do it! Do you have a ship captain training program?

Being out of a job as I presently am I know I would enjoy the job because it would be like combining work and pleasure. For one, you get to go to really nice places and meet many interesting people. Second of all, all the food is free, right?

Maybe I can start out on one of your smaller boats. I would rather not cruise to France but if it means getting the job I guess I have no choice.

Looking forward to hearing from you soon.

Sincerely,

Fred Grimes

Fred Grimes

FRED GRIMES

4087 San Rafael Avenue
Los Angeles, CA 90065

August 2, 1995

Jerold Ottley, conductor
The Mormon Tabernacle Choir
P.O. Box 112110
Salt Lake City, Utah 84147-2110

Dear Mr. Ottley:

I am writing so as to inquire whether being in the Mormon Tabernacle Choir is a paying
job. If so I would like to apply as I find myself temporarily unemployed.

I have heard you folks sing and boy you can sure blow the roof off! I do not have any
singing training but I am sure I can hold my own if you put me in the middle somewhere.
Even if I make a mistake everybody else sings so loud I am sure no one would hear me.

Mr. Ottley I am not Mormon. Is this a problem? If it is maybe I can think about changing
religions. I am not the most religious person in the world (references on request) so this
would not present a problem for me if it does not for you.

Also would I have to pay for the robe myself? This might present a problem.

Sincerely,

Fred Grimes

Fred Grimes

ONE MUST BE A MEMBER OF THE CHURCH WITH CONSIDERABLE
TRAINING AND VOCAL EXPERIENCE. ONE MUST ALSO LIVE IN THE SALT
LAKE AREA. THIS IS NOT A PAYING JOB — ALL VOLUNTEER.

FRED GRIMES

4087 San Rafael Avenue
Los Angeles, CA 90065

August 3, 1995

Cardinal Roger M. Mahony
Archbishop of Los Angeles
1531 W. 9th St.
Los Angeles, California 90015

Dear Cardinal:

I am exploring several job possibilities right now and would like to know whether I should consider being a priest.

It seems to me that priests do a lot of good work and get a lot of respect. Plus they get room and board and job security. The job security part means a lot to me as I recently lost my position down at the plant.

I am not Catholic but I do consider myself to be pure of heart (references on request) and in need of a job. I might be willing to convert if this is required.

My wife says I cannot be married and be a priest. Maybe we can work something out.

Please send me an application.

Sincerely,

Fred Grimes

Fred Grimes

Archdiocese of Los Angeles   Office for   1531   Los Angeles
Vocations   West Ninth   California
(213) 251-3248   Street   90015-1194

August 29, 1995

Fred Grimes
4087 San Rafael Avenue
Los Angeles, CA 90065

Dear Fred,

Thank you for your letter of August 3, 1995. The Cardinal has referred it to me because I am the director of Vocations.

Priesthood is not a job. It is one of the Christian <u>vocations</u> or <u>calls</u> from God. Marriage is another of the Christian vocations.

You indicated in your letter that you are married. So you have a vocation. I pray that you live out that vocation to the best of your ability with God's grace.

I regret that I am unable to encourage you toward the Catholic priesthood. Thank you for your interest. Please pray for priests. I will pray for you, especially during this time of unemployment as you seek work.

Sincerely yours,

Reverend Dick Martini
Director of Vocations

DM:ed

grimes.ltr
ed

FRED GRIMES

4087 San Rafael Avenue
Los Angeles, CA 90065

August 3, 1995

Mr. Daniel Goldin, administrator
NASA
300 E. Street S.W.
Washington, D.C. 20546

Dear Mr. Goldin:

Have you seen "Apollo 13?" The wife and I scraped together $14 and saw it the other night. Take it from me. Is it good. I thought those astronauts were goners for sure.

Sir why I am writing you is because I am looking for a job and was sort of thinking astronaut might be interesting. My friend Dave says it is a long shot me applying (no pun intended) to NASA but I thought I would go for it anyway. Do you have any openings?

I do not mean to take anything away from the astronauts you have now but those ones in the movie did not appear to do a very good job. They almost died. And that rocket ship they were flying. It could have crashed! I would be a lot more careful with government property. (references on request).

I am a little prone to airsickness but I see in the movie that so are some of the regular astronauts you have up there so I do not consider this too much of a problem. I could always take something for it.

Except for my back, I am in pretty good shape for my age. Also I enjoy travel so long as it does not involve France. I could always orbit over France if I had to.

Let me know.

Sincerely,

Fred Grimes

Fred Grimes

National Aeronautics and
Space Administration

Headquarters
Washington, DC 20546-0001

Reply to Attn of: P

Aug 10, 1995

Mr. Fred Grimes
4087 San Rafael Avenue
Los Angeles, CA 90065

Dear Mr. Grimes:

I am responding to your recent letter to NASA. I hope the enclosed information pertains to your request.

Your interest in the U.S. aeronautics and space program is greatly appreciated.

Sincerely,

Elsie Diven Weigel

Elsie Diven Weigel
Special Assistant for Communication
Office of Public Affairs

Enclosures

The 21st century promises the challenge for humans to live and work in space. The achievements of scientists, engineers, technicians, and specialists who will build and operate the Space Station are the legacy of the National Aeronautics and Space Administration's (NASA's) many years of experience in selecting and training astronauts to work on the frontier of space.

History of Astronaut Selection

Man's scope of space exploration has broadened since the first U.S. manned space flight in 1961. But the Nation can never forget the original seven space pilots who focused our vision on the stars. In 1959, NASA asked the U.S. military services to list their members who met specific qualifications. In seeking its first astronauts, NASA required jet aircraft flight experience and engineering training. Height could be no more than 5 feet 11 inches because of limited cabin space available in the Mercury space capsule being designed. After many series of intense physical and psychological screenings, NASA selected seven men from an original field of 500 candidates. They were Air Force Captains L. Gordon Cooper, Jr., Virgil "Gus" Grissom, and Donald K. "Deke" Slayton; Marine Lieutenant Colonel John H. Glenn, Jr.; Navy Lieutenant M. Scott Carpenter and Navy Lieutenant Commanders Walter M. Schirra, Jr., and Alan B. Shepard, Jr.

Each man flew in Project Mercury except Slayton, who was grounded for medical reasons. Sixteen years later, Slayton was an American crewmember of the Apollo-Soyuz Test Project, the world's first international manned space flight.

Nine pilot astronauts were chosen in September 1962, and fourteen more were selected in October 1963. By then, prime emphasis had shifted away from flight experience and toward superior academic qualifications. In October 1964, applications were invited on the basis of educational background alone. These were the scientist astronauts, so called because the 400-plus applicants who met minimum requirements had a doctorate or equivalent experience in the natural sciences, medicine, or engineering. Of these 400 applicants, six were selected in June 1965.

In April 1966, 19 pilot astronauts were named and in August 1967, 11 scientist astronauts were added to the program. When the Air Force Manned Orbiting Laboratory program was cancelled in mid-1969, seven astronaut trainees transferred to NASA.

Shuttle Era Astronaut Candidate Recruiting

The first group of astronaut candidates for the Space Shuttle Program was selected in January 1978. In July of that year, the 35 candidates began a rigorous training and evaluation period at NASA's Johnson Space Center (JSC), Houston, Texas, to qualify for subsequent assignment for future Space Shuttle flight crews. This group of 20 mission specialists and 15 pilots completed training and went from

astronaut candidate status to astronaut (active status) in August 1979. Six of the 35 were women and four were minorities.

Six groups of pilots and mission specialists have been added since then: 19 in 1980, 17 in 1984, 13 in 1985, 15 in 1987, 23 in 1990, and 19 in 1992.

Selection and Training for the Future

In the future, the United States with its international partners Japan, Canada, and the European Space Agency will operate a man-tended Space Station. From that orbiting depot, humans will continue their journeys to the Moon and Mars. As these plans become reality, the need for qualified space flight professionals will increase.

To respond to these needs, NASA accepts applications for the Astronaut Candidate Program on a continuous basis. Candidates are selected as needed, normally every 2 years, for pilot and mission specialist categories. Both civilian and military personnel are considered for the program. Civilians may apply at any time. Military personnel must apply through their parent service and be nominated by their service to NASA.

The astronaut candidate selection process was developed to select highly qualified individuals for human space programs. For mission specialists and pilot astronaut candidates, the education and experience requirements are at least a bachelor's degree from an accredited institution in engineering, biological science, physical science, or mathematics. Three years of related, progressively responsible professional experience must follow the degree. An advanced degree is desirable and may be substituted for all or part of the experience requirement (i.e., master's degree = 1 year of work experience, doctoral degree = 3 years of experience).

Pilot astronaut applicants must also meet the following requirements prior to submitting an application:

(1) At least 1,000 hours pilot-in-command time in jet aircraft; flight test experience is highly desirable.

(2) Ability to pass a NASA Class I space physical, which is similar to a military or civilian Class I flight physical and includes the following specific standards for vision: distance visual acuity - 20/50 or better uncorrected, correctable to 20/20, each eye.

(3) Height between 64 and 76 inches.

Mission specialists have similar requirements, except that the qualifying physical is a NASA Class II space physical, which is similar to a military or civilian Class II flight physical and includes the following specific standards for vision: distance visual acuity - 20/150 or better uncorrected, correctable to 20/20, each eye.

The application package may be obtained by writing to the Astronaut Selection Office, Mail Code AHX, Johnson Space Center, Houston, TX 77058-3696.

Applicants who meet the basic qualifications are evaluated by discipline panels during a week-long process of personal interviews, thorough medical evaluations, and orientation. The panel's recommendations are based on the applicant's education, training, and experience as well as

FRED GRIMES

4087 San Rafael Avenue
Los Angeles, CA 90065

August 3, 1995

Manny Jackson, owner
The Harlem Globe Trotters
1000 S. Fremont Ave.
Alhambra, California 91803-1349

Dear. Mr. Jackson:

I think your team is top drawer! Here is an idea that I think will help us both.

Hire me to play with the Globetrotters.

Yes. Me. Why hire an average unemployed American who is white to play with the best basketball players in the universe? Because it would be a first. Many people would come to watch the freak (me) but the joke would be on them because I would learn all the tricks before then and practice a lot and be just as good as the regular Globe Trotters!

I presently cannot shoot hoops to save my life. But I can whistle the heck out of Sweet Georgia Brown and that is a start, right?

Mr. Jackson I am unemployed having lost my job down at the plant so I can devote all my time and attention to this very exciting matter. The idea of playing with the Golbetrotters sends chills up my back. I am anxious to start. Just let me know.

Sincerely,

Fred Grimes

Fred Grimes

September 1, 1995

Mr. Fred Grimes
4087 San Rafael Avenue
Los Angeles, CA 90065

Dear Fred,

Thank you for your letter of August 3. We appreciate your interest in the Harlem Globetrotters.

Unfortunately, we will not be able to incorporate the "average unemployed American who is white" into our show at this time. As humorous as it might be, we have recently hired a performance director who has formatted the show for the next two years, and it does not include someone with your credentials.

You may however, begin honing your gymnastic skills, as we are always auditioning athletes for the position of Globie, our mascot.

Mr. Grimes, we will keep your letter on file, in case anything in our show changes. We thank you for your interest and continued support. Keep whistling!

Warm regards,

Colleen Lenihan

Colleen Lenihan
Assistant to Mannie Jackson

FRED GRIMES

4087 San Rafael Avenue
Los Angeles, CA 90065

August 5, 1995

Commissioner J.P.R. Murray
Royal Canadian Mounted Police
1200 Vanier Parkway
Ottowa, Ontario Canada K1AOR2

Dear Commissioner Murray:

Hello from down south.

I am writing to see about being a Mounty.

Ever since I was a kid I have always thought the Mounties were just about the best cops period. Racing around on dog sleds chasing bad guys has to be exciting. Plus your uniforms are the best.

I am not Canadian (references on request) but how different are you fellows from us anyway? Not much!

How do I sign up? What is the pay like? Also do I get my own dog?

I am really excited about this Commissioner. I hope you are too.

Sincerely,

Fred Grimes

Fred Grimes

Royal   Gendarmerie
Canadian   royale
Mounted   du
Police   Canada

PROTECTED "A"

1995-09-19

Mr. Fred Grimes
4087 San Rafael Avenue
Los Angeles, CA
90065
USA   95APB3219

Dear Mr. Grimes

We acknowledge receipt of your letter dated August 5, 1995

You will find attached an information package in regard to our basic qualifications in order to become a member of the Royal Canadian Mounted Police. You will also find attached other pertinent information in relation to the salary and the ten steps of our recruiting process. If you meet these basic qualifications, do not hesitate to contact us at area (613) 993-8259 or write to us at the undernoted address:

Royal Canadian Mounted Police
Recruiting Section
"A" Division
National Capital Region
250 Tremblay Road
Ottawa, Ontario
K1A 0R2

Your interest in the Royal Canadian Mounted Police is appreciated.

Yours truly,

Line April, Cst.
A. NCO i/c Recruiting Section
"A" Division
Ottawa, Ontario

FRED GRIMES

4087 San Rafael Avenue
Los Angeles, CA 90065

September 30, 1995

Line April, Cst.
Royal Canadian Mounted Police
A. NCO 1/c Recruiting Section
Ottowa, Ontario Canada

Dear Cst. April:

Thank you very much for getting back to me about my wanting to be a Mounty and all.

I looked real careful at the brochure you sent me especially the part about the job requirements. I think we have a little problem. The problem is I am not Canadian.

I know I meet the requirement that says you have to "be of good character" to be a Mounty. I have never been convicted of a felony. Ever. Plus I know I am "proficient in either of Canada's official languages." I know one of your languages is English which I speak real good (references on request). The other is French which I have no desire to speak. I would explain why not but we would be here all day.

Sir I realize this Canadian citizen thing could be a problem. If you could see it in your heart to make an acception to this rule I would be up there in a Montreal minute. I need the job!

Cst. April I will be looking to hear from you soon. Just out of curiosity, is it snowing up there already? We do not get much snow here as you may know.

Sincerely,

Fred Grimes

Fred Grimes

FRED GRIMES

4087 San Rafael Avenue
Los Angeles, CA 90065

August 6, 1995

Ms. Harriet Howard, Director Of Special Events
The Kentucky Derby
700 Central Avenue
Louisville, Kentucky 40208

Dear Ms. Howard:

I am toying with the idea of being a jockey in the Kentucky Derby and I hope you can help me.

I am not kidding anybody. I know that I will first have to be in a few other horse races before I ride in the Run For The Roses. But I really do not know who to ask about the particulars so I thought I would write you.

I have always liked horses. I rode one once when I was little. I am a little scared of heights but I did just fine. It was fun. Now that I am unemployed I figure why not combine business with pleasure.

Ms. Howard I am not the smallest man in the world (refereces on request). To be honest I would have to lose a lot of weight! But this is The Land of opportunity. If I thought I had a shot to ride in your fine race I would go on a diet right now and stick to it!

Ms Howard I am <u>serious</u> about this. What are my chances? Any advice you can offer would be much appreciated.

Sincerely,

Fred Grimes
Fred Grimes

FRED GRIMES

4087 San Rafael Avenue
Los Angeles, CA 90065

August 5, 1995

Thomas Grealish, president
LA-Z-BOY Chair Co.
1284 N. Telegraph Road
Monroe, MI 48161

Dear. Mr. Grealish:

I am in search of a new job having recently lost my position down at the plant. Last night as I was sitting there in the living room I had the idea that maybe I could work for your company to test your chairs one of which I have in my family room and think highly.

Sir do you have any employees in your plant who test the chairs by sitting and putting their feet up? I think this would be perfect for me. Not that I am a coach potatoe but I sure do enjoy my leasure time. So why not put it to productive use am I right?

I would be willing to come up and talk to you about this job. Just let me know. Maybe you could send me directions to Monroe "MI." I would be happy to drive. Do you reimburse for gas?

Thank you for your time.

Sincerely,

Fred Grimes

Fred Grimes

P.S.--I am not handicapped (references on request). My friend Dave is letting me use his computer to send out job letters. He said they should be "customized" to get more results. I tried to find a recliner in the "clip art" on the computer but the wheel chair was the best I could do. Thank you!

LA-Z-BOY®

October 26, 1995

Mr. Fred Grimes
4087 San Rafael Avenue
Los Angeles, CA 90065

Dear Mr. Grimes:

Thank you very much for your interest in our Company and your particular interest in being a "chair tester". Most of our testing is done using mechanical devices and only occasionally do we need a person to "test" the chairs for extended periods of time. At this time we are not seeking to fill this position.

Any testing positions that we would have available would be based at our Corporate Office in Monroe, Michigan.

We are certainly glad that you enjoy your current La-Z-Boy product and that you hold it in such high esteem that you would like to work for our Company.

Once again, thank you for your interest. I am sorry that I could not be of much help.

Sincerely,

LA-Z-BOY CHAIR COMPANY

Mark P. Lohman
Human Resource Manager
 Corporate Office

MPL:crp

Enclosures

LA-Z-BOY®

We Make The Rooms That Make A Home.™

FRED GRIMES

4087 San Rafael Avenue
Los Angeles, CA 90065

August 8, 1995

Mr. Lorne Michaels, producer
Saturday Night Live
NBC
30 Rockefeller Plaza
New York, N.Y. 10112

NO REPLY

Dear. Mr. Michaels:

How long do you figure your show has been on t.v.? A long time. You must be running out of guest hosts by now.

How about letting me host Saturday Night Live?

You are probably asking yourself right about now who is Fred Grimes? Just a hard working unemployed American one of billions trying to figure out a way to make a living after losing their job. If I hosted your show think of all the billions of ordinary people who would watch who are usually in bed when Saturday Night Live comes on. Your ratings would shoot up like they were back when you had the Killer Bees and those foreigners who sold Pepsi instead of Coke.

Mr. Michaels I can be funny. (references on request). The wife thinks I am a riot. Here is just a sample.

Q: What is this?: 10, 9, 8,7,6,5,4,3,2,1.
A: Bo Derek getting older.

How much does the host get paid?

Sincerely,

Fred Grimes

Fred Grimes

FRED GRIMES

4087 San Rafael Avenue
Los Angeles, CA 90065

August 5, 1995

Mr. Calvin Klein
Calvin Klein, Inc.
205 W. 39th St.
New York, N.Y. 10018

Dear Mr. Klein:

I will tell you something that could mean a lot more business for your company. Free.

Mr. Klein maybe you have not noticed it but all the men in your ads look like models. They are too good looking for the average American male such as myself to relate to. Mr. Klein nothing personal but who is making the decisions back there in N.Y.?

I would like to suggest that you hire me to be your head model. There are about a million men in America right now reading Sports Illustrated but do not buy your clothes because they cannot relate to these guys in your ads. Which is why most of us do not wear clothes from France. Who wants to look French? But if they were to pick up Sports Illustrated and see me an average unemployed working man (references on request) wearing your clothes everybody like me would probly run right out there are buy some because if I can look good in them they can too!

Mr. Klein I have applied for several jobs in N.Y. and expect to be getting some answers back pretty soon so I will not ask you to pay for the plane ticket back there to meet with you. But maybe you can go in halfs with some of these other places that I have applied for work. Like Macys Department Store. I have a good feeling about that one.

Well that is all I have to say for now. Mr. Klein I am looking forward to meeting you.

Sincerely,

Fred Grimes
Fred Grimes

FRED GRIMES

4087 San Rafael Avenue
Los Angeles, CA 90065

August 5, 1995

Mr. Gilbert N. Grosvenor, president
National Geographic Society
1145 17th St. N.W.
Washington, D.C. 20036-4688

Dear Mr. Grosvenor:

When I was a child I used to go down to the basement and sneak looks at the topless natives in your magazine. You probably did too. Let us face it. We all did.

Now that I am an adult I have discovered that I like the regular photography in your magazine. I think I am a pretty good photographer. The wife and my friend Dave think I have a talent. When we go on vacation I am the one who snaps the pictures (references on request).

Mr. Grosvenor I will not be going on vacation any time soon having lost my job down at the plant. I am looking for work. I would like to know if there are any photographer jobs available at your magazine. I would like to apply if so.

I know how tight money can be for equipment at companies today. Things down at theplant were pretty tight. I have my own camera so you would not have to buy me one if this helps. Plus I know a drug store that will develop film 2 rolls for 1.

I am enclosing a sample of my photography to give you an idea of what my abilities are. I hope you like it.

Please let me know about the job.

Sincerely,

Fred Grimes

Fred Grimes

National Geographic Magazine

1145 17TH STREET, NW

WASHINGTON, D.C. 20036-4688

KENT J. KOBERSTEEN
ASSOCIATE DIRECTOR OF PHOTOGRAPHY

August 22, 1995

Fred Grimes
4087 San Rafael Avenue
Los Angeles, CA 90065

Dear Mr. Grimes,

Thank you for your letter regarding photographic positions at the National Geographic.

While the National Geographic does have a small number of staff photographers, the majority of the photography in our publications is by freelance, rather than staff, contributors. It is also true that the competition for assignments is extremely keen. We are, I suppose, in the enviable position of being able to select from the world's best photojournalists. The majority of our assignments go to a relatively select cadre of staff, contract and freelance photographers.

Realistically, were we to add to the staff we would most likely do so from the ranks of the Contract Photographers. This fact, coupled with the great competition for relatively few assignments, makes it highly unlikely that someone with limited journalistic experience would receive assignments for our publications.

Many of the staff photographers now working for the Magazine have spent a number of years working for one or more of the better daily newspapers, as well as major magazines. Many of the freelance photographers who work for us also have considerable experience working for other national and international magazines.

If all this seems a bit negative, I apologize. It is, however, a response dictated by a rather precise goal for the look of the Magazine, coupled with a limited number of assignments.

Enclosed are the photographs you sent.

Thank you for your interest in the National Geographic.

Sincerely,

Kent Kobersteen

FRED GRIMES

4087 San Rafael Avenue
Los Angeles, CA 90065

August 6, 1995

Dave Letterman
CBS
51 W. 52nd St.
New York, NY 10019

Dear Dave:

Normally I do not watch you because you come on at 11:30 and working down at the plant you get up real early which means you go to bed real early so I don't watch you. But recently I lost my job so I was watching you.

You were talking about getting a lot of speeding tickets. Dave speed kills. You could be a menace to society if you are not careful! If you cannot drive safe then you need to find somebody who can. What about you letting me do the driving for you?

I am qualified. For one I live in L.A. Dave you should see the drivers here. Crazy does not begin to describe them. But in all the time I have been here I have had only two accidents and only <u>one</u> was my fault (references on request). Pretty good I would say.

I am a good listener. If I drove for you you could tell me all your jokes before you said them on t.v. That way you would know if they worked or not before you went on t.v. and pardon my French made an ass of yourself like you did the night I was watching you.

Well anyway that is my idea. Please get back to me soon as I am being considered for several jobs at present.

Sincerely,

Fred Grimes

Fred Grimes

P.S.--Don't get me wrong. I think you are funny.

39

FRED GRIMES

4087 San Rafael Avenue
Los Angeles, CA 90065

August 6, 1995

Mr. John Dalton, secretary of the Navy
The Pentagon
Washington, D.C. 20350

Dear Secretary Dalton:

I am thinking about joining the U.S. Navy. My problem is that I do not want just any job like mopping decks.

I am inquiring as to the possibility of being a SEAL.

I was a pretty good swimmer in high school. Plus I know a little bit about guns. My dad and me used to go out quite a lot and shoot bottles with the gun he brought back from the war. He used to call me "old dead eye." Not that I would ever want to shoot a person myself. But if it was a war I guess I would have to.

My friend Dave says I do not have a prayer of getting in. The wife and kids think I am nuts. But this is America. If you want something bad enough you can do it. And I want this! Also I am unemployed. I could really use a steady paycheck and I bet those boys make a lot of money.

Please send me information about pay uniform allowance etc. I will send you references on request.

Sincerely,

Fred Grimes.

DEPARTMENT OF THE NAVY
NAVY RECRUITING COMMAND
801 N. RANDOLPH STREET
ARLINGTON, VIRGINIA 22203-1991

IN REPLY REFER TO

1130
00132
31 Aug 95

Mr. Fred Grimes
4087 San Rafael Avenue
Los Angeles, California 90065

Dear Mr. Grimes:

This is in response to your letter of August 6, 1995 to Secretary Dalton requesting information about the Navy SEAL program.

Navy Recruiting Station Glendale personnel have been notified of your interest in the SEALs and can provide further information about Navy programs and answer any specific questions you may have about Navy SEALs. Please contact your Navy recruiter at (818) 242-2335.

Thank you for your interest in the Navy.

Sincerely,

O. W. DEMSKO
Head, Congressional and
 Special Inquiries Branch
By direction of the Commander

DEPARTMENT OF THE NAVY
NAVY RECRUITING STATION, GLENDALE
1415 E. COLORADO BLVD.
GLENDALE, CALIFORNIA 91205
(818) 242-2335

AUGUST 30, 1995

MR. FRED GRIMES
4087 SAN RAFAEL AVE
LOS ANGELES, CA 90065

DEAR MR. GRIMES:

YOUR LETTER TO MR. DALTON, SECRETARY OF THE NAVY, HAS BEEN FORWARDED TO THIS OFFICE FOR ACTION.

I AM YOUR NAVY REPRESENTATIVE. I NEED MORE INFORMATION FROM YOU TO DETERMINE IF YOU QUALIFY FOR THE U.S. NAVY SEALS.

PLEASE CALL ME AT (818) 242-2335 TO ARRANGE FOR A PERSONAL INTERVIEW TO DISCUSS YOUR FUTURE.

YOU AND THE NAVY,
FULL SPEED AHEAD
FT1/SS STEVEN SANDERS
NAVY RECRUITER

FRED GRIMES

4087 San Rafael Avenue
Los Angeles, CA 90065

September 2, 1995

FT1/SS Steven Sanders
Navy Recruiter
U.S. Navy
1415 E. Colorado Blvd.
Glendale, California 91205

Dear FT1/SS Sanders:

Thanks for writing me and being my Navy Representative. I would call but being without work I cannot afford a phone and my friend Dave is getting tired of me using his. I would drive over to see you but the bank took my car. I could take the bus but it would take three days probably.

To tell you the truth maybe my applying to the Navy is a bad idea. My friend Dave said he has a friend from high school who wanted to be a SEAL and the Navy guy said sure you can be a SEAL and when he finally promised to be in the Navy they put him on some ammo ship in the middle of no where and he spent four years mopping the floor!

Sir what I need to be doing is going full speed ahead not mopping floors. I have done that kind of work. I want to be better. If you cannot gurante that I will be a SEAL then I think I would be wasting my time and yours.

I hope I did not put you to to much trouble.

Sincerely,

Fred Grimes
Fred Grimes

FRED GRIMES

4087 San Rafael Avenue
Los Angeles, CA 90065

August 8, 1995

Daniel P. Tully, Chief Executive Officer
Merrill Lynch & Co.
World Financial Center
New York, N.Y. 10281

Dear Mr. Tully:

My Grandpa died awhile back and left me $1,200. I called up a stock broker and asked what I should do with so much money. He told me and guess what? I lost it all. I am not blaming him. He guessed that this one casino which is owned by Merv Griffin the talk show host was going to go through the roof and it went right in the crapper pardon the expression.

My point is I could guess better than that! So maybe I should be a stock broker. My friend Dave says all you guys do is guess anyway. I am good at guessing (references on request). I guessed last time the Dodgers won the series! It has been a while but I did not write you to talk about Baseball.

Mr. Tully your ads on t.v. say Merrill Lynch is bullish on America. I am not sure what that means but if it has anything to do with standing up for the Flag and supporting our great Country I am behind it 100 percent!

Mr. Tully I am unemployed and in need of a good job. Please send me an application. I will fill it out right away so we can both start making good money.

Sincerely,

Fred Grimes

Fred Grimes

Human Resources

World Financial Center
South Tower
New York, New York 10080-6111

 **Merrill Lynch**

August 21, 1995

Mr. Fred Grimes
4087 San Rafael Avenue
Los Angeles, CA 90065

Dear Mr. Grimes:

Your recent correspondence to Mr. Tully has been referred to me for consideration. We appreciate your considering career opportunities at Merrill Lynch.

We regret that at this time we have no positions available which would provide you with the experience you desire.

Your interest in becoming associated with us is greatly appreciated. We hope you will accept our good wishes for future success.

Sincerely,

Michele Coniglio
Vice President
Manager, Compensation & Recruiting

FRED GRIMES

4087 San Rafael Avenue
Los Angeles, CA 90065

August 9, 1995

NO REPLY

Senator Alan Simpson, R-Wyoming
Dirksen Senate Office Building Number 261
Constitution Avenue Between Delaware Avenue and 1st Street N.E.
Washington, D.C. 20510

Dear. Senator Simpson:

It seems like a lot of how my future is decided by people in Washington who do not have a real good grasp on what it is like for us regular people out here. Recently I lost my job down at the plant. I got me to thinking about ways I can make more money and have job security plus decide my own future. Why not be a Congress Man?

Sir the reason why I am writing to you is because you are from Wyoming and you were on one of those politics shows on Sunday morning that comes on before baseball. I checked my Road Atlas and there are not that many people in Wyoming which means there must not be that much competition to be a politican. I would like to know how I can get elected to Washington from there too.

Senator Simpson I am not out to take your spot so you can relax right now. The Senate seems too fancy for me. But the House looks like it mught be right up my alley. I was watching C-SPAN the other day and none of those Congressmen flapping their gums made a lick of sense! The wife says I would fit right in.

I have never been to Wyoming but I could always drive out there and spend a few weeks if I thought I had a shot at getting elected. I would bring my sleeping bag and sleep in a KOA campground. Can you please advise?

Sincerely,

Fred Grimes

Fred Grimes

FRED GRIMES

4087 San Rafael Avenue
Los Angeles, CA 90065

August 28, 1995

Ms. Barbara Eden
10100 Santa Monica Blvd. 16th Floor
Los Angeles, California 90067

Dear Ms. Eden:

I have been a fan of yours for as long as a I can remember.

When I was in high school, I had a Miss Jeanie picture up in my room. When I got married, you can imagine the wife was not real keen on the idea of it being up so down it came. But I never stopped being your fan.

Recently I lost my job down at the plant. I find myself out of work and looking. Call it a pipe dream but do you have a job that I might do for you? I could run errands or fix things around your house or whatever. I am not a weirdo or anything (references on request). Just a middle aged married guy who has admired you for a long time.

I have not discussed writing you with the wife but I am sure there would be no problem if you hired me as I am increasing need of a steady job which she does not hesitate to remind me all the time.

Well anyway I thought I would ask.

Sincerely,

Fred Grimes

Fred Grimes

P.S.--I saw you on t.v. the other day. You are as beautiful as ever.

FRED GRIMES

4087 San Rafael Avenue
Los Angeles, CA 90065

August 28, 1995

Ernest and Julio Gallo
P.O. Box 1130
Modesto, California 95353

Dear Ernest and Julio:

As far as I am concerned you make the best wine. Period! The wife and me do not have a lot of money to throw around and we have always found your wine to be a great value. We drink (sip) it all the time. References on request if you do not believe me.

Sirs, the reason I am writing you aside from letting you know I am a loyal customer is to inquire as to whether or not there might be any openings up there for "wine taster."

The fact of the matter is I am unemployed having lost my position down at the plant. So I am casting around hoping to land a good job. I was enjoying a glass of your fine Mountain Chablis last night when I thought hey why not apply.

Here is why I think I would be right for the job of taster.

* Enjoy wine
* Dependable and cheerful not snooty
* No "drinking" problem (would not swallow on the job)

How much would the job pay? Also would I be able to buy wine at a discount?

Thank you for your kind consideration.

Sincerely,

Fred Grimes
Fred Grimes

E. & J. GALLO WINERY

September 20, 1995

Mr. Fred Grimes
4087 San Rafael Ave
Los Angeles, CA 90065

Dear Mr. Grimes:

Thank you for your very kind and gracious letter. We do take considerable pride in our winemaking and are delighted to know of your preference for our wines.

Unfortunately, if we had a job of "wine taster" the applicant's line would indeed be quite long, Sorry!!

It was most thoughtful of you to take the time to write. We hope you continue to enjoy our fine wines for many years to come.

All the best,

E. & J. GALLO WINERY

Ms. Tedi Burris
Consumer Relations

TB/s

FRED GRIMES

4087 San Rafael Avenue
Los Angeles, CA 90065

August 30, 1995

The Amazing Kreskin
P.O. Box 1383
West Caldwell, New Jersey 07006

NO REPLY

Dear Kreskin:

I have a problem and I need your help in seeing into the future.

Sir I am out of work. I lost my job down at the plant. I decided one night I was not going to take another bad job so I have been sending out applications for really good jobs. Like astronaut and so forth. But so far all I am getting is a bunch of nos.

I can remember when you used to be on Johnny Carson and do all sorts of <u>amazing</u> things which is obviously why they named you that. I have not seen you on the tv lately but I hope you are doing good and making a comeback. Sir can you tell me if I am going to get any of these jobs I am applying for or is a waste of time and effort etc etc?

I would be happy to pay you what little I can for your services. The wife took me to one of these palm readers over on Melrose and they wanted fifty bucks which I cannot afford as I am out of work which I guess I already said.

Anyway I realize you are a long way away over there in New Jersey but can you give it a try. Please?

Sincerely,

Fred Grimes

Fred Grimes

FRED GRIMES

4087 San Rafael Avenue
Los Angeles, CA 90065

September 15, 1995

Mr. Jimmy Carter
One Woodland Drive
Plains, Georgia 31780

Fred – Thanks for your idea. When all the poor have homes, we can start on the rich. —

Jimmy C

Dear Mr. President:

First let me say sir that I have always been a big fan of yours. Even when you made everybody turn down the temperature in their house to save energy I was behind you.

Recently I saw you on t.v. putting up houses for the poor. Sir my hat is off to you. What you are doing building these houses for poor people is a good thing. But Mr. President I think I have an idea that could benefit a lot of other people including yourself.

Sir why not build houses for the rich? You could call them "Jimmy Carter Homes" or "Homes By Jimmy Carter." I bet a lot of rich folks would buy them just to tell to tell their friends, "Guess who hung my dry wall?" I do not know how pea nut farming is doing these days but I bet you and your lovely wife could make a lot more money and maybe even pay for another run for the White House if you built houses for the rich!

Mr. President I am making this suggestion to you because I am unemployed and would like to be your construction foreman. I am pretty handy around my own house (references on request) if I do say so myself. For what it is worth I put a new sink in the kitchen just last week!

Thank you for your time and attention to this matter. I am looking forward to hearing from you.

Sincerely,

Fred Grimes

Fred Grimes

FRED GRIMES

4087 San Rafael Avenue
Los Angeles, CA 90065

September 15, 1995

Mr. Jim West, executive director
International Chili Society
P.O. Box 2966
Newport Beach, California 92663

Dear Mr. West:

I bet you and I would agree there is nothing better in this world than a good bowl of chili. Am I right?

Sir the reason I am writing you is to inquire as to whether you may have any openings in your office for the position of chili taster. I am presently unemployed and exploring several new job possibilities. As I like chili an awful lot I decided why not combine business with pleasure.

Mr. West I think I would be perfect for the job. For one I have an iron stomach. For another I really do like chili! I like it with eggs, hot dogs, bagles. You name it. I also make chili. My neighbors say it is the best (references on request). If I get the job I will tell you the secret ingredients.

I am available at your convenience for an interview whenever you want. Just let me know.

Sincerely,

Fred Grimes

Fred Grimes

INTERNATIONAL CHILI SOCIETY

September 18, 1995

Mr. Fred Grimes
4087 San Rafael Avenue
Los Angeles, CA 92663

Dear Fred:

　　Thanks for your letter I am sure you would be a great taster. Right now that job is filled and we have a waiting list.

　　Good luck to you and "keep your pot hot."

Sincerely,

Jim West
Executive Director

FRED GRIMES

4087 San Rafael Avenue
Los Angeles, CA 90065

September 15, 1995

Barbara Boxer, U.S. Senator
2250 E. Imperial Highway Suite 545
El Segundo, California 90245

Dear Senator Boxer:

As my constituent I need your help.

Recently I lost my job down at the plant. Even though I am a working man I like to write poetry (references on request). I found out there is a job called "Poet Laureat." I wrote to Newt Gingrich asking if he knew anything about it and whether the position was filled, etc. etc. He never even got back to me!

Are you people back there in Washington so out of touch with us "regular" folks that you do not even have the courtesy to write back when we are trying to better ourselves??? Senator I do not mean to blame you for Mr. Gingrichs bad attitude. But I can tell you what. I would never vote for him for President that is for sure!

Senator I realize you are a busy person but could you help me? I just want to know who I can send in an application to and make something of myself instead of working down at the plant the rest of my life.

Sincerely,

Fred Grimes

Fred Grimes

P.S.--Also can you find out how much the job pays? Thank you!

BARBARA BOXER
CALIFORNIA

COMMITTEE ON ENVIRONMENT
AND PUBLIC WORKS

COMMITTEE ON BANKING,
HOUSING, AND URBAN AFFAIRS

COMMITTEE ON THE BUDGET

JOINT ECONOMIC COMMITTEE

DEPUTY WHIP

United States Senate

HART SENATE OFFICE BUILDING
SUITE 112
WASHINGTON, DC 20510–0505
(202) 224–3553

1700 MONTGOMERY STREET
SUITE 240
SAN FRANCISCO, CA 94111
(415) 403–0100

2250 EAST IMPERIAL HIGHWAY
SUITE 545
EL SEGUNDO, CA 90245
(310) 414–5700

525 B STREET
SUITE 990
SAN DIEGO, CA 92101
(619) 239–3884

2300 TULARE STREET
SUITE 130
FRESNO, CA 93721
(209) 497–5109

September 27, 1995

Fred Grimes
4087 San Rafael Ave.
Los Angeles, CA 90065

Dear Mr. Grimes:

Thank you for writing to me regarding the position of poet laureate of the United States. In May of this year Mr. Robert Haas was appointed poet laureate by the Library of Congress. His term of service is one year. The position pays $35,000 per year. He replaces Rita Dove.

Mr. Haas is a poet, scholar and educator of national renown. He is currently on faculty at U.C. Berkeley and also teaches at the University of Iowa's prestigious writer's workshop. He has published three poetry collections.

The duties of the poet laureate specifically include reading from his or her works upon assuming and leaving the job and organizing programs of readings at the Library. Poet Laureates usually act directly and symbolically to encourage the creation and appreciation of American verse. Of probable interest to you, the appointment of Mr. Haas, the first poet laureate from the Western United States, promises to place more emphasis on West Coast poetry at the Library than in years past.

Mr. Haas and his predecessors did not apply for this position. Candidates are recommended by their work, their colleagues and their potential to inspire in others a respect, if not reverence, for what can be one of the most sublime and democratic forms of human expression.

Thank you again for writing. I wish you the very best of success in finding a suitable outlet for your poetry.

Sincerely,

Barbara Boxer
United States Senator

BB/jo

FRED GRIMES

4087 San Rafael Avenue
Los Angeles, CA 90065

September 19, 1995

Glenn Bacheller
Baskin-Robbins Ice Cream
31 Baskin Robbins Place
Glendale, California 91201

Dear Mr. Bacheller:

I have taken the family to eat your ice cream at least a million times. That is how much we love it. My favorite used to be fresh peach but I have not seen it lately on your 32 flavors list. But that is not why I am writing.

Sir I am unemployed. I would like to know whether or not you have any openings for the position of ice cream taster?

I think this would be a great job. I think I would be perfect for it. For one I love ice cream I could eat it all day long (references on request). For another I know good ice cream when I taste it and Mr. Bacheller you have good ice cream!

If the taster job is not open I could always be like an advisor to you. Here is one idea I have. Get rid of the regular cones and just give people the sugar ones. No offense but the regular cones taste like a UPS box.

As I live close by I could take the bus over at any time for an interview with you. Just let me know.

Sincerely,

Fred Grimes

Fred Grimes

Baskin-Robbins Incorporated
Corporate Headquarters
31 Baskin-Robbins Place
Glendale, CA 91201
Phone: (818) 956-0031

September 21, 1995

Mr. Fred Grimes
4087 San Rafael Avenue
Los Angeles, CA   90065

Dear Mr. Grimes:

Your letter directed to Glenn Bacheller has been forwarded to my office for consideration and review.

We will evaluate your experience and background in relation to any available positions we currently have open. Should an appropriate position be available or become available, we will contact you. In the meantime, we will be happy to keep your letter on file.

Thank you for considering Baskin-Robbins as a prospective employer.

Sincerely,

Suzanne Ferguson
Manager, Employee Relations
Human Resources Department

FRED GRIMES

4087 San Rafael Avenue
Los Angeles, CA 90065

September 20, 1995

Walter Armatys, executive director
Toy Manufacturers of America, Inc.
200 Fifth Avenue
New York, New York 10010

Dear Mr. Armatys:

You must have the best job in the world. Getting to play with toys all day. We should all be so lucky.

Sir I am writing so as to inquire about whether or not you might have any toy tester jobs available.

I am very experienced in this area. I have children. Pardon the expression but it seems like we have toys coming out the wazoo. Most of these toys I myself have put together (references on request). Here is one idea I have. Stop giving kids toys that have a million parts most of which get stuck in the vacume cleaner or eaten by the dog. The kid winds up crying and all you want to do is get in your truck and keep driving if you know what I mean.

Mr. Armatys I am out of work. I could be available to start testing toys immediately.

I am looking forward to hearing from you soon.

Sincerely,

Fred Grimes
Fred Grimes

**TOY MANUFACTURERS
OF AMERICA, INC.**

200 FIFTH AVENUE
NEW YORK, NY 10010
PHONE 212/675-1141
FAX 212/633-1429

September 25, 1995

Mr. Fred Grimes
4087 San Rafael Avenue
Los Angeles, CA 90065

Dear Mr. Grimes:

Your letter was of September 20 was forwarded to me; Walter Armatys retired more than seven years ago.

As we are a trade group and not a toy manufacturer (see page 3 of the enclosed Fact Book), we do not test toys. Most toys are tested in professional independent testing labs by trained engineers. However, as you indicated that you have invented toys, I am enclosing our toy inventor/designer guide as a reference.

Best of luck.

Sincerely,

Jodi Levin
Communications Director

FRED GRIMES

4087 San Rafael Avenue
Los Angeles, CA 90065

September 15, 1995

Mrs. Vigdis Finnbogadottir
Office of the President
Reykjavik, Iceland

NO REPLY

Dear President Finnbogadottir:

Greetings from America! It is about 90 degrees here. I hope it is not too cold where you are but I bet it is.

Mrs. Finnbogadottir the reason I am writing you is because I was flipping through the phone book the other day looking for a concrete company to come fill up the pool in the backyard as we can no longer afford it and I noticed the heading "Consulates & Other Foreign Government Representatives." Being unemployed I have time on my hands so I went through the list. Mrs. Finnbogadottir maybe I am wrong but it looks like Iceland is just about the only country that does not have an office in L.A.

You need a representative here if I may say so. Someone who can tell people in California about all the great things about Iceland and make them want to go to Iceland for vacation and spend money. I would like to put in the for the job.

Mrs. Finnbogadottir I could lie to you and tell you I am part Icelander but I do not think I am (references on request). To tell you the truth I do not know much about Iceland. But I can learn. Which is what being American is all about.

Sincerely,

Fred Grimes

Fred Grimes

P.S.--I do not know if you speak English up there or not but I sure hope you do.

FRED GRIMES

4087 San Rafael Avenue
Los Angeles, CA 90065

September 25, 1995

Seiji Ozawa, conductor
Boston Symphony Orchestra
Symphony Hall
Boston, Massachusetts 02115

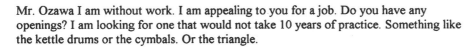

Dear Mr. Ozawa:

Boy can you guys play.

Mr. Ozawa I am without work. I am appealing to you for a job. Do you have any openings? I am looking for one that would not take 10 years of practice. Something like the kettle drums or the cymbals. Or the triangle.

Sir let me be honest. I have never seen the orchestra play. When you are a working man and are out of work like I am at the present it is kind of hard to afford good seats. Also I do not play any musical instruments at present. But I have been listening a little to you play on the radio and I think this is definitely something I can do.

Mr. Ozawa I am very good at taking direction. Just ask anyone down at the plant (references on requests). I would be very careful and when you told me to ding the triangle or whatever I would do it!

Would I have to pay for my own instrument? This could present a problem. Also what is the pay like?

I could always drive out there for an interview if you were inclined.

Sincerely,

Fred Grimes
Fred Grimes

FRED GRIMES

4087 San Rafael Avenue
Los Angeles, CA 90065

September 25, 1995

Mr. Dick Clark
3003 W. Olive Avenue
Burbank, California 91505

Dear Mr. Clarks:

I love American Bandstand! My friends and me used to watch it all the time. I have not seen it on t.v. for some time. Is it still on? If so what are chances of me being a dancer on American Bandstand. It looks like fun.

Mr. Clark let me be up front with you. I am not a professional dancer. The wife and I go dancing once every blue moon. But I think this makes me the perfect candidate to be on American Bandstand!

Everybody on the show is young and beautiful and really gets down! They know all the moves. But how about having a typical middle aged out of work guy (references on request) out there cutting a rug? I could help bring back all the old dances like the mashed potatoe and the monkey. Mr. Clark they probably would not admit to it but I bet a lot of folks my age watch your show. If you hired me the word would spread that one of "there own" was on American Bandstand. Your ratings would go up for sure!

I am dependable and ready to go!

Sincerely,

Fred Grimes
Fred Grimes

dick clark

productions, inc.

3003 WEST OLIVE AVE. BURBANK, CA 91505-4590
(818) 841-3003   FAX: (818) 954-8609

September 27, 1995

Thanks so much for your kind letter, Mr. Grimes.

I'm afraid that you are a little late with your
request. American Bandstand went off the air in
1989. Rest assured, however, if the show were
still running, we would have loved to have had you
join us!

Thanks, again, for thinking of us.

Sincerely,

Dick Clark

DC/as

Mr. Fred Grimes
4087 San Rafael Avenue
Los Angeles, CA 90065

FRED GRIMES

4087 San Rafael Avenue
Los Angeles, CA 90065

September 25, 1995

Kenneth Feld, president
Ringling Brothers and Barnum & Bailey Circus
P.O. Box 2366
Washington, D.C. 20026

Dear Mr. Feld:

I have been giving this a lot of thought and I have decided I want to be in the circus.

There was a story in the paper the other day about clown tryouts. Well forget that. I am afraid of clowns. Particularly the ones with orange hair. Sometimes I have bad dreams that they are stomping me with those big feet.

Maybe you can tell me what openings you have and I can write back and let you know if I am qualified. I will tell you that getting shot out of the cannon is not a good idea as I hurt my back down at the plant before I became unemployed. Plus I am a bit afraid of heights. So I guess that rules out the high wire.

One thing I might be good at is the lions. We have a cat that gets pretty wild sometimes and I am always having to "tame" him. This usually means me throwing him out the back door and letting him think about things for a while before he gets to come back inside. Anyway, I like cats a lot if this helps you.

Mr. Feld I really need a good job. I hope you can help.

Sincerely,

Fred Grimes

Fred Grimes

January 17, 1996

Fred Grimes
4087 San Rafael Ave.
Los Angeles, CA 90065

Dear Mr. Grimes,

We are delighted to hear of your interest in performing with Ringling Bros. and Barnum & Bailey Circus. Working with The Greatest Show On Earth involves a lot of hard work and dedication, but it can be a truly unique and rewarding experience. Since you have an interest in animals, we have some recommendations on training them.

At Ringling Bros. and Barnum & Bailey Circus, our family simply wouldn't be complete without the wonderful animals who perform and travel side by side with us. Every member of The Greatest Show On Earth cares deeply about the welfare of these magnificent creatures.

As you already know, taking care of any animal is an enormous responsibility. Our trainers spend up to 16 hours a day with their animals - not just training them, but feeding them, grooming them, and playing with them. Gaining an animal's trust is much more important than teaching him a trick. With patience, sensitivity, and positive reinforcement, you can build this trust, and training can become a mutual delight for you and your pet. Our most famous animal trainer, Gunther Gebel-Williams, can stand in the middle of an arena and, simply by using his voice, command 18 elephants simultaneously. Gunther's animals respect him because Gunther respects his animals.

If you keep some of these thoughts in mind when you work with your pet, you'll be on the right track. Enclosed are materials on the Circus. Best of luck, and May All Your Days Be Circus Days!

Sincerely,

Jody Clay
Media Center

FRED GRIMES

4087 San Rafael Avenue
Los Angeles, CA 90065

October 13, 1995

Mr. Andre Moriaillon, manager
Office of French Tourism
444 Madison Avenue
New York, New York 10022

Dear Mr. Moriaillon:

Bonjour.

Some years ago the wife and I went on our honeymoon over to your country. To say it was a distaster would be putting it mildly. For one we could barely speak with your people over there. For another nobody seemed to care one bit about what Americans want or need when they are in a foreign land. Things like ice cubes and cheese burgers. You don't even have French Toast.

Mr. Moriaillon not to be insulting but we made a decision never to go to France again. Especially after some of our neighbors went. They said the people they met over there were you guessed it. Snooty.

What you need sir is somebody like me on your staff who can help educate France as to the ways of Americans. This way Americans will be happier and spend more money which will make France a lot more happy I am sure.

Here is one suggestion I am giving you. For free. The French still enjoy lighting up after a meal of petits or whatever. Sir, most of us over here have quit smoking and find having smoke in our face over supper rude and inconsiderate.

So how about it? I would like to apply for the job of American advisor to France. What do you think?

Sincerely,

Fred Grimes

Fred Grimes

FRED GRIMES

4087 San Rafael Avenue
Los Angeles, CA 90065

October 20, 1995

Mr. Andre Moriaillon, manager
Office of French Tourism
444 Madison Avenue
New York, New York 10022

Dear Mr. Moriaillon:

Today in the mail I received an envelope from your office. In it was the letter I sent you a week or so ago asking if you had any jobs available on your staff for an American advisor.

Mr. Moriaillon I am a little confused. Maybe you meant to send me a response to my letter and by accident sent me back my letter instead? No problem if so. I certainly make my share of mistakes every day!

Sir I would still very much like to work for your organization if there are any openings. If you could see fit to getting back to me one way or another I would sure appreciate it.

Merci!

Sincerely,

Fred Grimes

Fred Grimes

FRED GRIMES

4087 San Rafael Avenue
Los Angeles, CA 90065

October 28, 1995

The Playboy Advisor
Playboy
680 North Lake Shore Drive
Chicago, Illinois 60611

Dear Sir:

I have always enjoyed your magazine. One part I have not always understood is The Playboy Advisor. All these guys writing about all their sex problems and asking questions about their scrotums etc. etc. My friend Dave says the letters are all made up like the bodies of the Playmates but I do not believe that for one second!

The problem as I see is not the letters but your answers. For example "S.L" from Savannah Georgia wrote last month that he had heard some doctors can do vasectomies without cutting on you and you said yes this is correct they can now "puncture" your gonads with a forceps and be done with it. Sir I knew a guy down at the plant who had this done and he swolled up to the size of a grapefruit! (references on request). This is the kind of thing that should at least be mentioned in Playboy don't you think??

How about me an average American helping answer the letters for you? When some guy writes about running into some kinky girl who likes having sex with him and her Doberman or whatever, I would set him straight. Dump her like a hot rock and get the hell out of there. Fast.

Please consider this my application for the job.

Sincerely,

Fred Grimes
Fred Grimes

PLAYBOY

November 8, 1995

Mr. F. Grimes
4087 San Rafael Ave.
Los Angeles, CA 90065

Dear Fred:

We have a very long list of "average Americans" who'd like to
help us with the Advisor. Most of them, however, don't realize
just how hard this job is; apparently, like Cal Ripken and
baseball, we make it look much easier than it really is. We
don't make up answers; we rely on experts and a variety of
opinions to draw conclusions. Occasionally, our experts goof, or
we omit a fact or a valid point--but we'd like to think that's
the rare exception. In any case, we'll keep your application on
file.

Thanks for your interest in PLAYBOY.

Sincerely,

Mark Williams

Mark Williams
for the Playboy Advisor

MW/mo

FRED GRIMES

4087 San Rafael Avenue
Los Angeles, CA 90065

October 5, 1995

Mr. Jack LaLanne
P.O. Box 1023
San Luis Obisbo, California 93406

Dear. Mr. LaLanne:

Recently the wife bought one of these "Buns of Steal" exercise tapes. I do not know if you have seen this tape but basically it has a lot of models in leotards with very tight "buns" stretching this way and that way and clapping their hands and generally acting like they are on stage in Las Vegas. The wife watched about 10 minutes and put it away.

Sir what people in this country need is a hero who can get them off the couch and make them do good old jumping jacks for 2 hours, a hero who is so strong he can pull a locomotive with his teeth. Mr. LaLanne that hero is you.

I used to watch you on t.v. when I was younger (references on request) and I was never in better shape in my entire life! Mr. LaLanne how about coming out of retirement and get another show on t.v.? I will be your "before" and "after" model. I will do the jumping jacks. I will do the squat thrusts. And when you are done with me I will look great.

I recently lost my job down at the plant so am available right away. Maybe we could do some stretching and talk about the salary, benefits, etc. etc.

Sincerely,

Fred Grimes

Fred Grimes

FRED GRIMES

4087 San Rafael Avenue
Los Angeles, CA 90065

November 2, 1995

Judge Lance Ito
210 West Temple Street
Department 103
Los Angeles, California 90012

Dear Judge Ito:

Sir my hat is off to you. You were so fair in the trial of Mr. O.J. Simpson that it made me proud just to be an American. If I ever got in trouble with the law which I have never been thank goodness (references on request) I would want you to be my judge.

Would you be interested in coming to supper at my house?

Judge Ito the reason I am asking is two reasons. First I think you did a great job and deserve a good meal. The wife says she will fix you <u>anything</u> you want. You do not know how rare that is. She has never said this to me in all the years we have been married. Second I would like to talk to you about any openings you may have on your staff as I would like to work for you.

Let me say up front sir that I am not a lawyer and never want to be but Judge watching you up there in that big chair day in and day out made me see that being a judge could be a wonderful job. I figure if I am going to be one why not learn from the best right? Sir this is why I am writing you. Judge Ito you are the best judge in America as far as I am concerned!

As I am presently unemployed my schedule is wide open. If you would let me know when you would like to come over to eat we can set it up! Just give me a couple days head start so the wife can go to the store first. Sir it would be an honor to have you in my house.

Sincerely,

Fred Grimes

Fred Grimes

FRED GRIMES

4087 San Rafael Avenue
Los Angeles, CA 90065

November 8, 1995

Linda J. Walton, editor
Cats Magazine
P.O. Box 290037
Port Orange, Florida 32129

Dear Ms. Walton:

How do I get my cat in your magazine?

His name is Roy. He is a good cat. I am not sure what breed he is, to tell you the truth.
Just a cat. But he never sharpens his claws on the sofa. Also he is the only cat I have ever
seen that will actually eat leftover salad with Wishbone Italian dressing on it. Which makes
him pretty "purrfect" in my book. (get it?)

Ms. Walton the point I am trying to make is that I have seen your magazine and you spend
a lot of time and attention on "fancy" cats. Probably 99% of the people in this country
who have cats have regular cats. Cats that will not win no beauty contests. Like Roy. Why
not spend more time on them?? Think of all the new subscriptions you would sell.

As I am presently unemployed (references on request) with no other real time
commitments at present I would be happy to arrange a photo shoot for Roy.

Just out of curiosity, how much does something like this pay?

Sincerely,

Fred Grimes

Fred Grimes

CATS
MAGAZINE

December 8, 1995

Fred Grimes
4087 San Rafael Avenue
Los Angeles CA 90065

Dear Mr. Grimes:

In response to your letter about how to get your cat Roy into CATS Magazine, I enclose our writers' and photographers' guidelines for your perusal.

Your observation that *CATS Magazine* does not spend much space on "regular" cats and spends too much time on "fancy" cats is not very accurate, in my opinion. Perhaps you've missed seeing the many stories, poems and photographs sent in by our readers, which are selected without regard to whether the cat in question is purebred or a mixed breed. Perhaps you did not see our August 1995 issue, which focused on helping feral cats. We also publish various columns and articles with information of interest to friends of felines of all types. We do have a regular feature called *Breed of the Month*, but that one feature per issue does not constitute the whole focus of our magazine.

A closer examination of *CATS Magazine* on your part may be in order before you submit material to be considered for publication. We advise all potential contributors to our magazine to familiarize themselves with the content and focus of our publication.

Sincerely,

Becky Bridges

Becky Bridges
Assistant Editor

FRED GRIMES

4087 San Rafael Avenue
Los Angeles, CA 90065

November 3, 1995

Arthur Cooper, editor
GQ Magazine
350 Madison Avenue
New York, New York 10017

Dear Mr. Cooper:

I believe I have a way that you can sell a lot more magazines.

Mr. Cooper please do not take offense at this but most of the men in America do not dress the way they do in your very fine publication. Most of us either can not afford this sort of fancy clothes or would feel silly wearing them or both. I am not saying that you should not show these clothes because I am sure a lot of men in New York wear them and that is fine. But a lot of the guys I worked with down at the plant before I lost my job would not be caught dead in them (references on request).

Sir how about devoting a part of your magazine to what the average man wears? You could call it "Duds" or what ever. I would be happy to write this column. Each month could be a new topic. Here are just a few ideas I have:

1. Pictures and sayings on T shirts--cool decoration or free advertising?
2. Socks--do we really need them?
3. Old Jeans--at what point do you toss them?
4. Sneakers (see No. 2).
5. Underwear (see No. 3)

Mr. Cooper I am sure you would agree this kind of column could attract a lot more readers. I would be happy to talk with you further. Just let me know.

Sincerely,

Fred Grimes
Fred Grimes

FRED GRIMES

4087 San Rafael Avenue
Los Angeles, CA 90065

November 8, 1995

Donna Robinson, director
American Society of Dowsers
Danville, Vermont 05828

Dear Ms. Robinson:

I am thinking of being a dowser. What is the job market like?

I have a knack for finding water. At least once a month I run over a sprinkler head with the lawn mower and next thing you know it looks like Old Faithful in my backyard (references on request).

But seriously my friend Dave had a leak in the water line the other day leading in from his water meter. He did not know where. For the heck of it I grabbed a branch from his tree and aimed. Darned if that branch did not start pulling me to a spot in the lawn. I dug down about three feet and sure enough, there it was. A leak. Actually I was off by about five feet but the point is I found it eventually. Which led me to think about dowering as a line of work that might be good for me.

What is the pay like? And benefits? Are some sticks better than others? If there is a staff position available in your office I would like to apply for it. Ms. Robinson I am unemployed having lost my job down at the piant so I could start any time.

Thank you for your prompt attention to this vital matter.

Sincerely,

Fred Grimes
Fred Grimes

FRED GRIMES

4087 San Rafael Avenue
Los Angeles, CA 90065

November 9, 1995

James. R. Corbett, president
Bike Athletic Company
P.O. Box 666
Knoxville, Tennessee 37901

Dear Mr. Corbett:

As a leading manufacturer of jock straps, I have an idea that I think could make us both a lot of money: designer jock straps.

Sir I am very serious about this. Take a look at men's underwear today. It used to come in two models and one color. White jockeys and white boxers. Now they are every color you can imagine and every fit. You and I both know that somebody is buying all this underwear and somebody is making money off them!

Mr. Corbett please do not take this personally but it is like your company has not kept up with modern times. I went to the sporting goods store the other day and noticed that your jock straps look exactly like they did when I used to wear them (references on request). Sir you could be losing big money!

As I am presently unemployed I would be happy to work for your company bringing jock straps into the 21st century. Here is one idea I have: make some paisley, striped, etc. etc. Make some silk! Take a look at your average Penneys or Sears and see how many of the men's underwear they sell are paisley or silk. A lot!

I do not have any experience in clothing design but I think enthusiasm counts for something, don't you?

Sincerely,

Fred Grimes

Fred Grimes

FRED GRIMES

4087 San Rafael Avenue
Los Angeles, CA 90065

November 13, 1995

Stan Lee, publisher
Marvel Comics
387 Park Avenue South
New York, New York 10016

NO REPLY

Dear Mr. Lee:

I have what I think is an exciting idea that could bring fresh "blood" to the world of super hero crime fighters: The Amazing Superdad.

Yes Superdad. He could be a regular guy. The kids do not know he is Superdad. Just Dad. The only time he uses his Super Powers around the house is when he has to mow the lawn or clean out the garage etc. etc. He kicks it into "dad gear" and can go 800 mph doing all the chores when nobody is looking. Only Roy the family cat knows his true powers. But at night after everybody goes to bed Superdad and Roy get up and gets in his car called the Dad Defender. It looks like a 1979 Monte Carlo but it has a secret button that can turn it into a sort of stealth fighter. Superdad and trusty Super Roy go and duke it out with evil bad guys all night keeping the world safe. Then they come back home before dawn and nobody even knows they have been gone! Sometimes Superdad has to go out during the day. He always tells his family he is going down to "bowl a few frames" or is taking Roy to the vet but they are really going out to keep the world safe!

Mr. Lee you can imagine how popular this idea could be. Every kid in America who reads your comics would see his Dad in a new light! I do not have any experience writing or drawing comics (references on request) but I would like to write Superdad. As I am presently unemployed my schedule is wide open.

Mr. Lee what do you say?

Sincerely,

Fred Grimes

Fred Grimes

FRED GRIMES

4087 San Rafael Avenue
Los Angeles, CA 90065

November 13, 1995

Robin Leach, host
Lifestyles Of The Rich and Famous
875 3rd Avenue #1800
New York, New York 10022

Dear Mr. Leach:

I know you are probably on some luxurious beach in the Pacific doing another story on beautiful people drinking champane and diving off waterfalls etc. etc. but I thought I would write you with what I think is an idea you would really like.

Sir the fact is that most people can not afford to go jetting off to all these far away places you have on your show. Forget the airfare. One night alone in one of these fancy hotels is more than my entire mortgage payment! Maybe the lovely Donna Mills has money to burn. But most Americans including myself do not.

So why not do a show about us? You could call it "Lifestyles of the Average American" or something like that. Show the way people <u>really</u> live. Going to the bowling alley or the galleria on a hot summer night to escape the heat or just sitting out in the backyard with the neighbors and a case of cold ones. Mr. Leach I am here to tell you that billions of people would watch this kind of show.

Not to be forward or anything but maybe you could do the first show on me. I am just a hard working unemployed American who lost his job down at the plant and has been looking for work now for months (references on request). After that I could help line up other regular folks to feature on your show. I just know it would be a hit!

So what do you say Mr. Leach? There is a whole market just waiting to be tapped. How about we do it together?

Sincerely,

Fred Grimes

Fred Grimes

FRED GRIMES

4087 San Rafael Avenue
Los Angeles, CA 90065

November 13, 1995

Dennis Phelps, president
Clowns of America, Inc.
P.O. Box 570
Lake Jackson, Texas 77566

Dear Mr. Phelps:

Recently I wrote to Ringling Brothers about joining up with the circus. They did not even have the common decency to write me back so now I am writing you.

Sir I am considering going into your line of work. I would like to know if you know of any clown jobs out there.

While I do not have no experience in this area I am confident I would make a good clown. For one the wife says I am naturally funny looking (references on request). I feel this could be an advantage. Also I have pretty good balance so if I was to use stilts or those big orange feet in my act I would not be tripping all over the place and landing on innocent people at least not on accident.

I got a go cart in the garage that has not worked for years. I am thinking of fixing it up and using it for my Clown Mobile. Sir would you know if this type of vehicle requires any special licenses in other states? Here in California you better believe it does! Also if you have any tips on how to get makeup off. I was experimenting last weekend with some of the wife's stuff and it took <u>forever</u> to get it off me. I finally had to use a mixture of dish soap and 409 Cleaner. Talk about painful. How do the pros do it?

Sincerely,

Fred Grimes

Fred Grimes

P.O. Box 570
Lake Jackson, TX 77566
December 29, 1995

Fred Grimes
4087 San Rafeal Ave.
Los Angeles, CA 90065

Dear Mr. Grimes:

We are in receipt of your letter requesting membership information. Attached is a Membership Application. If you are interested, please complete, attach your check or money order (in U.S. funds only), and send to the address shown above. One new form of membership is now available, *"LIFE"* membership for a one time fee of $300.00.

Membership in COAI includes our 48+ page magazine *"THE NEW CALLIOPE,"* which contains numerous articles on the art of clowning, makeup application, costuming, skit development and implementation, and tips for clowning in different situations. It also has advertisements for all types of clown equipment, makeup, and costumes. Clown workshops are listed in the calendar for the coming year.

Fred, clowning is a serious business and it takes special training to do it correctly. In our magazine there are several schools advertised that could get you started. Oh, by the way use baby oil and shampoo to get make-up off. If you don't have baby oil then any oil will do, motor, machine, olive, etc. or butter, cold cream, make-up remover, but not 409!

I hope to hear from you soon.

Yours in clowning,

David "Shorty" Barnett
Business Manager
Clowns of America International

FRED GRIMES

4087 San Rafael Avenue
Los Angeles, CA 90065

November 13, 1995

Idi Amin
Ruler In Exile Of Uganda
Box 8948
Jidda 21492, Saudi Arabia

Dear Mr. Amin:

It has been a while since I saw you in the news but I assume you are doing as best as can be expected being in exile and all from your beloved and beautiful homeland.

Sir I have an exciting idea for you. Have you given any thought to having a public relations company represent you to improve your public image? I am ready willing and able to be your public relations representative to the American People. Being an American myself (references on request) I know what Americans like and do not like. Together I bet we can improve your image 1,000%!

As you know Americans are not big on dictators. You know what Americans like? Sweaters. You should wear them more often and arrange for photo opportunities for the press. They would make you look like a regular guy. Also maybe you can start a fund raising drive while you are there in Saudi Arabia waiting to return to Uganda. Toys for Tots always needs donations. Or Jerry Lewis. Sir people would love you!

Mr. Amin I would be happy to talk with you further about this very exciting idea and my very reasonable fee.

Sir I am looking forward to being your spokesman in America.

Sincerely,

Fred Grimes
Fred Grimes

FRED GRIMES

4087 San Rafael Avenue
Los Angeles, CA 90065

November 16, 1995

Ray Colonna, executive director
United States Lifesaving Association
425 E. McFetridge Drive
Chicago, Illinois 60605

Dear Mr. Colonna:

Have you ever watched Bay Watch on t.v.? I am sure Pamela Anderson has done as much to make lifeguarding a popular job as Mr. Spock did for space travel. But even though I do not have experience at lifeguarding I thought I would put in for it and see what happens.

Sir do you have any openings or know of any lifeguarding jobs around?

I think this could be a real good job for me. For one I like to swim (references on request). I am not afraid of deep water. I am a little afraid of big waves and sharks. Probably everybody is right? Also I have always enjoyed going to the beach and looking at all the lovely "scenery" if you know what I mean. I burn just like a lobster but I think I would be okay if I wore a t-shirt at all times and a straw hat. I would take the hat off if I had to go in and save somebody's life.

I know I am probably wasting my time looking for a lifesaving job but as I am unemployed I have a lot of time to waste. Any help you could swing my way would be much appreciated.

Sincerely,

Fred Grimes

Fred Grimes

FRED GRIMES

4087 San Rafael Avenue
Los Angeles, CA 90065

December 1, 1995

Kathy Bartels, director
Barbara Eden's Official Fan Club
P.O. Box 5556
Sherman Oaks, California 91403

Dear Ms. Bartels:

What is the deal with Barbara Eden???

Being a huge fan of hers as I am sure you are I sent her a letter back in August to what I was told was her address. I wanted to see if she might be interested in me working for her. Like fixing things around her house or trimming the hedges. Anything. I am not a weirdo or anything. Just an unemployed fan who has seen every episode of I Dream of Jeanie at least 3 times.

Anyway the letter came back unopened! This is not the Barbara Eden I know. And I am sure it is not the one you know either.

What gives? Can you please find out for me if she needs any help around the house. If so I would be happy to provide references on request and start right away.

Sincerely,

Fred Grimes

Fred Grimes

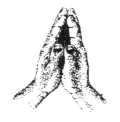

FRED GRIMES

4087 San Rafael Avenue
Los Angeles, CA 90065

November 16, 1995

Jimmy Swaggart
P.O. Box 2550
Baton Rouge, Louisiana 70821

Dear Mr. Swaggart:

I know it has been a while since you were on the t.v. but I still think of you. Sir you were just about the best evangelist on Sunday mornings in my book. I hope you are doing well.

Jimmy you made some mistakes in your life but so what? Sir everybody makes mistakes. The Good Book tells us that he who has sinned should not throw stones. So why are people throwing stones at you?? Yes Jimmy you got caught with a prostitute. Big deal. So do millions of guys probably every day. Sir I think people should get off your back. I think you should be back on t.v. spreading the Good Word!

Jimmy let me be honest if I may. I am unemployed. I have been looking for a job for quite a few months now and nothing seems to be working right. I got to thinking about being a preacher but I do not have the faintest idea where to start looking for work in this field. You being the best and all I am hoping you can give me some pointers. I am not particular about religions if this helps (references on request). I would be willing to preach to just about any religion so long as it does not involve animal sacrifice, voodoo etc., etc.

Do you know of any jobs or how much they pay. I have a good suit and could start at any time.

Jimmy, God bless you and yours!

Sincerely,

Fred Grimes

Fred Grimes

FRED GRIMES

4087 San Rafael Avenue
Los Angeles, CA 90065

December 1, 1995

Michael J. Connor, commissioner
Professional Bowler's Association of America
1720 Merriman Road
Akron, Ohio 44313

Dear Mr. Connor:

When I was working down at the plant a lot of the guys would go bowling on Wednesdays after shift break. Usually I would have to get home to mow the yard help the kids with their projects etc. etc. But I did start going and last time I bowled a 210 (references on request). I have been practicing and my average is getting up there. Now that I am unemployed I am thinking about maybe trying to be a professional bowler.

Sir I am wondering if there are any sponsors out there who would be willing to sponsor me. This could be a good deal for them. They could get a lot of stories in the press about how they sponsored a "regular" guy. A lot of other regular guys would get fired up and go out and buy the sponsors products!

My friend Dave is letting me borrow his ball so I do not even need to buy one. I could probably buy my own shoes depending on how much they cost but I thought I would wait to hear from you in the hope that maybe if you knew of a sponsor they would give me a pair or at least loan me some shoes.

Mr. Connor thank you in advance for getting back to me as soon as possible.

Sincerely,

Fred Grimes

Fred Grimes

Professional Bowlers Association

1720 MERRIMAN ROAD • P.O. BOX 5118 • AKRON, OHIO 44334-0118

216/836-5568   FAX 216/836-2107

Dec. 6, 1995

Mr. Fred Grimes
4087 San Rafael Ave.
Los Angeles, Calif. 90065

Dear Fred:

This is in response to your letter regarding the sponsoring of Professional Bowlers
Association (PBA) members.

Most of our professionals have individual sponsors. Many are family members or local
businesses that have taken an interest in that bowler. Our players acquire these sponsors
on their own. PBA does not seek sponsors for individual bowlers.

Thank you for your letter and best regards.

Sincerely,

PROFESSIONAL BOWLERS ASSOCIATION

Bobby Dinkins
Director of Operations

FRED GRIMES

4087 San Rafael Avenue
Los Angeles, CA 90065

December 23, 1995

Frederic W. Hills, senior editor
Simon & Shuster
1230 Avenue of the Americas
New York, New York 10020

Dear Mr. Hills:

My name is Fred Grimes. I think you should publish a book about my life.

I have never walked on the Moon or anything. I am just a regular joe who used to work down at the plant and is now unemployed. I love my wife and kids and do not cheat on my taxes. Once I accidentally stabbed myself in the leg with a hunting knife. It is a long story that I would save for the book.

Mr. Hills you may be saying "Well, so what? Who would buy a book about a guy like that aside from his family." A lot of people that's who. Sir who says you have to be rich or famous to have a book or movie about you? My story is the story of the common man. I have been a golf caddie. I have poured driveways. I have installed chain link fence. And I had a good job down at the plant. I got married had kids and bought a house. It is no palace but I am proud of it. If the bank does not foreclose, we will own it in about 29 years. What will things be like then I wonder!

A lot of people would relate to my story . It would be a best seller. Everybody would say, "Boy. That Fred is just like me. I feel better about myself knowing some regular guy could get a book on his life. If he can do it so can I!" I have plenty of pictures to go with the book. Also references on request.

I have not yet written the book. The idea hit me just this morning as I was thinking of a new way to put bread on the table. My friend Dave said he would let me borrow his computer to write it.

I am ready to get to work. Just let me know!

Sincerely,

Fred Grimes
Fred Grimes

SIMON & SCHUSTER

Simon & Schuster Consumer Group
1230 Avenue of the Americas
New York, NY 10020
212-698-7350

Frederic W. Hills
Vice President
Senior Editor

Simon & Schuster
Touchstone
Fireside

January 22, 1996

Fred Grimes
4087 San Rafaei Avenue
Los Angeles, CA 90065

Dear Mr. Grimes:

Thanks for your letter of December 23, which I read with interest. In the end, though, there was not enough enthusiasm among my colleagues here to publish your project successfully.

Good luck with it in any case.

Sincerely,

Frederic W. Hills

FRED GRIMES

4087 San Rafael Avenue
Los Angeles, CA 90065

December 19, 1995

Mr. Andre Moriaillon, manager
Office of French Tourism
444 Madison Avenue
New York, New York 10022

Dear Mr. Moriaillon:

I wrote to you looking for a job and you sent me back my letter with no response whatsoever. I wrote you back figuring maybe you made an honest mistake. But I still have not heard from you. I can only assume that you are too busy eating goose liver on crackers and sipping chianti or shopping for berets to get back to a regular American such as myself.

Sir with this kind of attitude is it any wonder that we Americans think you French folks are rude and snooty? How can you act this way when you are a visitor in my country? How can you act this way when the United States of America bailed your wimpy little country out of not one but two count 'em, TWO, World Wars??? Wars in which some of my own personal relatives participated even though they ended up on Guam which I know is a long way from France but I think you get the point.

Mr. Moriaillon I have about had it up to here with your rude behavior. Forget I ever applied. I would <u>never</u> work for your snooty little organization. I have instructed the wife that we will no longer be eating French toast on Sunday mornings in our house! We will no longer be pardoning our French and I will make very sure from now on that when she goes to the grocery store, she does not buy any box wine from France!

And I damn sure will not be going to France to spend my hard earned dollars anytime soon.

Have a nice day.

Sincerely,

Fred Grimes

Fred Grimes

FRED GRIMES

4087 San Rafael Avenue
Los Angeles, CA 90065

January 25, 1996

Patricia Ireland
National Organization For Women
1000 16th Street N.W. Suite 700
Washington, D.C. 20036

Dear Ms. Ireland:

I would like to work as a consultant for your organization.

I am not a woman. I am just a regular guy who used to work down and the plant. But I know a fair amount about women, not only being the product of one fine lady but being married to one (references on request). I think women are the best! Sometimes The Wife gets on my nerves a little and vise versa but what marriage doesn't right?

Being a male I believe I can give you the male perspective on important subjects. This way when you are trying to get Congress to listen to you you will know in advance exactly what all those Congressmen are thinking! Same with the President and Senators. Think how much more successful your efforts will be to promote womens rights, etc. etc.

Ms. Ireland I do not mean to criticize but sometimes I think your organization takes themselves too seriously. Not that what you are doing is not important. But I just feel that maybe you can attract more flies with honey than with vinegar as my Mother is fond of saying. This is also where I could come in handy. If you hired me to be a consultant I could help lighten things up a little. Who knows. Maybe even men would start joining.

Sincerely,

Fred Grimes

Fred Grimes

P.S.--I believe in equal pay for equal work. Enclosed please find $5 to help further the cause.

FRED GRIMES

4087 San Rafael Avenue
Los Angeles, CA 90065

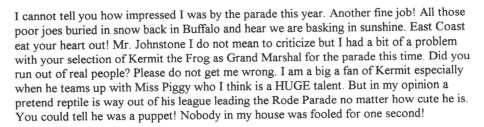

January 29, 1996

Bill Johnstone, president
Tournament of Roses Parade
391 S. Orange Grove Boulevard
Pasadena, California 91184

Dear Mr. Johnstone:

I cannot tell you how impressed I was by the parade this year. Another fine job! All those poor joes buried in snow back in Buffalo and hear we are basking in sunshine. East Coast eat your heart out! Mr. Johnstone I do not mean to criticize but I had a bit of a problem with your selection of Kermit the Frog as Grand Marshal for the parade this time. Did you run out of real people? Please do not get me wrong. I am a big a fan of Kermit especially when he teams up with Miss Piggy who I think is a HUGE talent. But in my opinion a pretend reptile is way out of his league leading the Rode Parade no matter how cute he is. You could tell he was a puppet! Nobody in my house was fooled for one second!

I would like to make a suggestion. What you need is a regular person to be Grand Marshal. At the risk of sounding like I have a big head which I do not (references on request) I would like to nominate myself. Why should you consider me? Well for one thing I am an ordinary guy. Being unemployed I would have lots of time to train for the next Parade. If you picked me it would be an inspiration to billions of other ordinary guys who watch every year. For what it is worth I am pretty strong so my arm would not get tired waving. Also I live close by. Which means you would not have to fly me in and put me up at some swanky hotel (although I think it is safe to say TheWife and me would not turn down a free night at the Ramada).

What are the pay and benefits like for Grand Marshall?

Sincerely,

Fred Grimes
Fred Grimes

FRED GRIMES

4087 San Rafael Avenue
Los Angeles, CA 90065

January 30, 1996

NO REPLY

Penny DiCamillo, producer
The Rockettes
Radio City Music Hall
1260 Avenue of the Stars
New York, New York 10020

Dear Ms. DiCamillo:

I have admired the Rockettes for about as long as I can remember. What are the chances of being one?

The Rockettes are about the best dancers in the world pound for pound that I have ever seen. When they get into that big line at the end and start high kicking all together and the audience goes crazy it makes my heart beat a little faster. It used to amaze me that they did not hurt each other kicking like that but then I realized how good they are!

Ms. DiCamillo I should tell you that my dancing experience is not the most extensive (references on request). The truth is I have never danced professionally. But I do consider myself a real fast learner. If you gave me the chance I would work so hard you would not believe it. My hamstrings are a little tight right now but they would loosen up as soon as I got back into a regular exercise program I am sure.

Please provide me information on salary, benefits, costume allowance etc. etc.

Sincerely,

Fred Grimes

Fred Grimes

P.S.--Where do you get all those feathered hats? They are <u>awesome</u>!

FRED GRIMES

2001 Grand Avenue
Santa Barbara, California 93103

August 9, 1996

Mark G. Gearan, director
Peace Corps
Esplanade Building
1990 K. Street, N.W.
Washington, D.C. 20526

Dear Mr. Gearan:

Do you remember President Kennedy who said ask not what you can do for your country but what you can do for your country? I think JFK was just about the best President we ever had in my opinion don't you? I don't pay any attention to that Marilyn Monroe stuff. Who could blame him anyway.

Mr. Gearan to get to the point I am looking for a job and I wondered if you had any good ones available? By good I mean jobs in places where I would not have to sleep with water buffalo and wash my clothes in some river if you get my drift.

Sir let me be right up front with you. I think the Peace Corps is doing a great job helping the world and everything. I would like to help the world too but I have gotten a little too used to my creature comforts (references on request) I must admit and the last thing I want to do is camp out for a year with a bunch of head hunters and eat goat or whatever just to teach them to read English.

Does the Peace Corp have any jobs in places like England or Cancun? I would not be interested in working in France because I personally do not think they appreciate the fact that we bailed them out of World War One and World War Two.

Mr. Gearan how much does the job pay and what kind of benefits are there?

Sincerely,

Fred Grimes

Fred Grimes

PEACE CORPS
DIRECTOR

August 15, 1996

Mr. Fred Grimes
2001 Grand Avenue
Santa Barbara, CA 93103

Dear Mr. Grimes:

Thank you for your interest in becoming a member of the Peace Corps staff.

The Office of Human Resource Management only accepts employment inquiries for specific vacancies, so I have enclosed a complete list of current staff vacancies. You can obtain more detailed Vacancy Announcements that describe the qualification standards and job responsibilities more thoroughly by calling the toll free number (800 818-9579) or by writing:

> Peace Corps
> Office of Human Resource Management
> 1990 K Street, N.W. - Room 4100
> Washington, DC 20526

I encourage you to submit a separate application for each position of interest. You may want to request a list of Vacancy Announcements every few weeks from our Office of Human Resource Management to keep abreast of new vacancies as they occur.

Good luck with the job search.

Sincerely,

Mark D. Gearan
Director

Enclosure

Peace Corps Office of Human Resource Management
1990 K Street NW, Room 4100 • Washington, DC 20526

CURRENT STAFF VACANCIES LISTING: August 12, 1996

This is only a listing. Refer to the Vacancy Numbers below when calling for Vacancy Announcements: 1-800-818-9579, TDD: (202) 606-0086. For information on becoming a Peace Corps Volunteer, please call Toll Free: 1-800-424-8580. Current Peace Corps employees, regardless of geographic area, are eligible to apply for all positions. Applications must be postmarked by the closing date and must be received within five (5) days after the closing date. Applications may be submitted via facsimile (fax) machine, 202-606-9410, no later than the closing date. Print/type your name on each page.

DOMESTIC VACANCIES with APPLICATION DEADLINES:

Vacancy Number	Closing Date	Title Series-Grade (GS equivalent)	Organization Location	Consideration
PC6-094	08-19-96	Regional Recruiter FP-301-07/05 (GS-07/09)	San Francisco Regional Office San Francisco, CA	Nationwide
PC6-100	08-19-96	Programming and Training Officer FP-301-4/3	Ecam/Headquarters Washington, DC	Worldwide
PC6-106	08-19-96	Country Desk Assistant FP-303-7/6 (GS-303-7/8)	Inter-America Headquarters Washington, DC	DC Commuting Area
PC6-110	08-19-96	Computer Specialist FP-33404/3 (GS-11/12/13)	Office of Information Resources Management Washington, DC	All Sources
PC6-105	08-23-96	Chief of Operations FP-340-02/01 (GS-14/15)	Africa Region Washington, DC	Peace Corps Employees Only
PC6-112	08-23-96	Administrative Support Assistant FP-303-07 (GS-07)	Associate Director/ Management Washington, DC	DC Commuting Area
PC6-113	08-23-96	Program Analyst FP-343-07 (GS-07)	Associate Director/ Management Washington, DC	Peace Corps Employees Only
PC6-107	08-26-96	Budget Analyst FP-560-5/4 (GS-560-9/11/12)	Asia Pacific Headquarters Operations Washington, DC	DC Commuting Area
PC6-111	08-26-96	Program Assistant FP-303-7 (GS-303-7)	Ofc. of Administrative Services Washington, DC	DC Commuting Area
PC6-114	08-26-96	Executive Secretary FP-318-7/6/5	ECAM Washington, DC	DC Commuting Area
PC6-115	08-26-96	Country Desk Officer FP-301-5	Ecam/Headquarters Washington, DC	Peace Corps Employees Only
PC6-104	09-03-96	Auditor FP-511-4/3 (GS-11/12/13)	Office of Inspector General Washington, DC	Worldwide
PC6-109	09-10-96	Business Development Spec. FP-1101-5/4/3	Ofc. of Training and Program Support Washington, DC	Worldwide

Update: 8/12/96

FRED GRIMES

2001 Grand Avenue
Santa Barbara, California 93103

August 16, 1996

Mark G. Gearan, director
Peace Corps
Esplanade Building
1990 K. Street, N.W.
Washington, D.C. 20526

Dear Mr. Gearan:

Thank you for sending me all your job openings. I sat down and took a look at them real close like you said. About the only one that looked interesting to me was "country desk officer." I was not sure but I figured maybe the job had something to do with being in the country and sitting at a desk all day. Having spent a long time working down at the plant on my feet all day with all the smoke and noise that sounded pretty good let me tell you! I got pretty excited until I found out you could only apply if you were already working at the Peace Corps. Plus it requires a college degree. Oh well.

Sir let me cut right to the chase. Do you have any paying jobs for an average American that do not require any heavy lifting in any of the following areas.

1. Honolulu Hawaii.

2. Cancun Mexico or Bahamas.

3. London England.

I am a good American and could represent my Country to the fullest!

Sincerely,

Fred Grimes

Fred Grimes

FIRST CLASS

2001 Grand Avenue
Santa Barbara, California 93103

August 9. 1996

Marvin Runyon, Post Master General
United States Postal Service
475 L'Enfante
Plaza West, S.W.\
Washington, D.C. 20260

Dear General:

The other day I went to the post office to get some stamps. They were out of the sticky ones so I had to buy the ones you lick. I stuck them on some job application letters I was sending out. On the envelopes I mean. And it got me to thinking. Why not have stamps in different flavors?

Think about it. You could have stamps that tasted like rocky road ice cream. Or a vodka tonic. People would buy stamps just to lick them. You would make more money and have fewer mail to ship all over the place!

Sir I am giving this idea to you free because I am full of these kinds of valuable ideas (references on request). Do you have any openings on your staff for an idea man? I recently lost my job so I could start any time.

Here is another idea I am giving away: why not have stamps with the faces of baseball players. You know how popular baseball trading cards are among the younger kids? People could collect stamps for the same reason. Or how about movie stars? Have you ever thought about a stamp of Elvis Presely? There are lots of fans of Elvis still out there even though he is dead and if these people buy Elvis sweat (truth!) I bet they would buy Elvis stamps like crazy! The trick here is to get people to <u>buy</u> stamps but not <u>use</u> them. This way, you make money and have less work to do!

I hope these ideas I have given you a sense of how important I could be working as an idea man for you. General, I am looking forward to speaking with you soon.

Sincerely,

Fred Grimes

Fred Grimes

UNITED STATES
POSTAL SERVICE

August 20, 1996

Mr. Fred Grimes
2001 Grand Ave
Santa Barbara, CA 93103-1926

Dear Mr. Grimes:

This responds to your August 9 letter to Postmaster General Runyon.

Our commemorative stamp program is a big money-maker for us. There are an estimated 20 million stamp collectors in the United States who purchase a large number of commemorative stamps and never claim the delivery service represented by the stamp. As a consequence, annually, the revenue the Postal Service receives from stamps retained by collectors and from other philatelic products is $250 million. Since this revenue is applied against the general operational costs of the Postal Service, it benefits all mailers.

We sold 41 billion stamps in 1995 with Marilyn Monroe being the top seller. In 1993, Elvis Presley won the honors and remains the all-time most popular stamp sold in our history --124 million saved.

Our Manager, Stamp Services oversees our stamp program and distribution and production. The Citizens' Stamp Advisory Committee reviews about 40,000 yearly public suggestions for our stamp designs and makes recommendation to Mr. Runyon. Some 100 stamps are issued each year. Enclosed is the criteria used in making selections. Living baseball players are ineligible for a stamp. Our committee works three(3) years in advance and now working on 1999 program. Your ideas would be welcome by writing the committee directly.

Adhesive used today on our stamps is edible and biodegradable as it has a cornstarch base that is water activated. The glue is food grade, water soluble, and approved by the FDA. Being ever conscious of many health problems/allergies our customers suffer, the allergic effect some flavors and colorants may pose has deterred us from offering flavored stamp glue as you suggest. We have elected to keep our glue neutral in taste. For those who dislike the taste, we now offer our very popular self-adhesive stamps which can be peeled and affixed.

We appreciate your interest in our stamp program.

Sincerely,

Connee L. Rainey
Senior Consumer Affairs Associate

Enclosure
Reference:62280048:lkm
475 L'ENFANT PLAZA SW
WASHINGTON DC 20260-2200
202-268-2284
202-268-2304

2001 Grand Avenue
Santa Barbara, California 93103

August 9. 1996

Connee L. Rainey, Senior Consumer Affairs Associate
United States Postal Service
475 L'Enfante
Plaza West, S.W.\
Washington, D.C. 20260

Dear Ms. Rainey:

How about a stamp of Dick Clark?

Sincerely,

Fred Grimes
Fred Grimes

UNITED STATES POSTAL SERVICE

August 30, 1996

Mr. Fred Grimes
2001 Grand Ave
Santa Barbara, CA 93103

Dear Mr. Grimes:

I'm in receipt of your August 9 letter and suggestion we consider a stamp in honor of "Dick Clark".

What a great idea and no doubt be popular but unfortunately prohibited as no living person may be portrayed on a U.S. stamp per enclosed CSAC criteria.

Your interest is most appreciated.

Sincerely,

Connee L. Rainey
Senior Consumer Affairs Associate

Enclosure

475 L'ENFANT PLAZA SW
WASHINGTON DC 20260-2200
202-268-2284
202-268-2304

101

FRED GRIMES

2001 Grand Avenue
Santa Barbara, California 93103

August 9, 1996

Rodney E. Slater, administrator
Federal Highway Administration
400 Seventh Street, S.W.
Washington, D.C. 20590

Dear Mr. Slater:

I am guessing that a busy man such as yourself does not have a lot of time to get out there and inspect the highways and byways in this fair Land of ours. Assuming this is true, I am wondering if you have room on your staff for a person to cruise the country and make sure the highways work o.k.

I did a fair amount of driving all over the country before I had a Wife and Kids and a job and so forth. I still have the Wife and Kids but the job went south if you know what I mean. So now I am looking for a new line of work and I thought this might be a good idea.

What I could do is drive around sort of wherever the road took me. Or where ever you wanted me to go. Sort of like a roving inspector. You could pay me a salary and a reasonable allowance that would cover my mileage and room and board in the Ramada or Holiday Inn on the governments dime. Admission to water slides and alligator exhibits etc. etc. I would pay for myself of course. I could telephone you whenever I found a problem like pot holes or whatever and you could send a crew to fix it. Think of the millions of people this would help!

I have my own car so I could save the government some money right there. Plus I am not a big breakfast eater so you would only have to spring for two meals per day.

Mr. Slater what do you think?

Sincerely,

Fred Grimes
Fred Grimes

U.S. Department
of Transportation

**Federal Highway
Administration**

400 Seventh St., S.W.
Washington, D.C. 20590

August 29, 1996

Mr. Fred Grimes
2001 Grand Avenue
Santa Barbara, California 93103

Dear Mr. Grimes:

Thank you for your inquiry concerning employment opportunities with the Federal Highway
Administration (FHWA). Your letter to Federal Highway Administrator, Rodney E. Slater
has been forwarded to our office for reply.

We appreciate your interest in the National Highway System; however, we have no positions
for which you may be considered. The FHWA works in cooperation with State and local
governments to administer programs such as highway design, research and development, and
safety. The majority of our positions are in technical areas such as civil engineering,
transportation planning, and safety management.

The State Department of Transportation Agencies perform highway maintenance activities.
You may want to contact the State Department of Transportation in California to learn about
what needs they may have for someone with your experience. Their address is Department of
Transportation, P.O. Box 942873, Sacramento, California, 94273-0001, and the phone number
is 916-654-5266.

To assist you with your Federal job search, you may wish to contact the Office of Personnel
Management's (OPM) Federal Job Information Center nearest the location where you desire to
work. The OPM offices will be able to provide you with information on Federal job
opportunities with other Federal agencies. Enclosed is a directory of OPM offices located
throughout the U. S.

We appreciate your interest in the FHWA and wish you success.

Sincerely yours,

George S. Moore, Jr.
Associate Administrator for
Administration

Enclosure

U.S. Office of Personnel Management
Federal Employment Information Centers

ALABAMA: Huntsville 🖳 520 Wynn Dr., NW., 35816-3426, 24 Hour Telephone Service: (205) 837-0894, Telephone Service: M-F/8-4, Staff on Duty: M-F/8-1, Self-Service: M-F/1-4

ALASKA: Anchorage 🖳 222 W. 7th Ave., #22, Rm. 156, 99513-7572. Callers in Alaska: (907) 271-5821, Staff on Duty: T-Th/11-1. Callers outside Alaska: (912) 757-3000.

ARIZONA: (See NEW MEXICO)

ARKANSAS: (See San Antonio, TX)

CALIFORNIA: Los Angeles 🖳 9650 Flair Dr., Suite 100A, El Monte, 91731, 24 Hour Telephone Service: (818) 575-6510, Self-Service: M-F/8-5

Sacramento 1029 J St., Rm. 202, 95814, (415) 744-5627, Self-Service: M-F/8-4

San Diego 🖳 Federal Building, Rm. 4260, 880 Front St., 92101, (818) 575-6510, Self-Service: M-F/8-5

San Francisco 120 Howard St., Suite B. For mail only: P.O. Box 7405, 94120, 24 Hour Telephone Service: (415) 744-5627, Self-Service: M-F/8-4

COLORADO: Denver 🖳 12345 W. Alameda Pkwy., Lakewood, 24 Hour Telephone Service: (303) 969-7050. For mail only: P.O. Box 25167, 80225, Staff on Duty: M-F/12-3:45, Self-Service: M-F/9-12

CONNECTICUT: (See Boston, Massachusetts), For Touch Screen Service, see reverse.

DELAWARE: (See Philadelphia, PA)

DISTRICT OF COLUMBIA: 🖳 Washington, DC, Metropolitan Area, Theodore Roosevelt Fed. Bldg., 1900 E St., NW., Rm. 1416, 20415, Staff on Duty: M-F/8-4, 24 Hour Telephone Service: (202) 606-2700

FLORIDA: Miami Claude Pepper Federal Building, Rm. 1222, 51 SW. 1st Ave., Self-Service: M-F/8:30-4, (Walk-in only. For mail or telephone, see Georgia listing)

Orlando 🖳 Commodore Building, Ste. 125, 3444 McCrory Place, Self-Service: M-F/9-4, (Walk-in only. For mail or telephone see Georgia listing).

GEORGIA: Atlanta 🖳 Richard B. Russell Federal Building, Rm. 940A, 75 Spring St., SW., 30303, 24 Hour Telephone Service: (404) 331-4315, Telephone Service: M-F/ 8:30-4, Staff on Duty: M-F/9-1, Self-Service: M-F/7-5

HAWAII: Honolulu 🖳 (and other Hawaiian Islands and Pacific overseas): Federal Building, Rm. 5316, 300 Ala Moana Blvd., 96850, Callers in Hawaii: (24 Hour Telephone Service) (808) 541-2791, Staff

on Duty: M-F/9-12. Callers outside Hawaii: (912) 757-3000.

IDAHO: (See Seattle, WA)

ILLINOIS: Chicago 🖳 230 South Dearborn Street, Room 2916, 60604, 24 Hour Telephone Service: (312) 353-6192, Staff on Duty: M-F/8-4:30, (For Madison and St. Clair Counties, see St. Louis, MO, listing)

INDIANA: (See MICHIGAN), (For Clark, Dearborn, and Floyd Counties, see Ohio listing), For Touch Screen Service, see reverse.

IOWA: (See Kansas City, Missouri), 24 Hour Telephone Service: (816) 426-7757, (For Scott County, see Illinois)

KANSAS: (See Kansas City, Missouri), 24 Hour Telephone Service: (816) 426-7820

KENTUCKY: (See OHIO), (For Henderson County, see Michigan)

LOUISIANA: New Orleans 🖳 1515 Poydras St., Ste. 608, 70112, 24 Hour Telephone Service: (210) 805-2402, Self-Service: M-F/8-5

MAINE: (See Boston, Massachusetts), For Touch Screen Service, see reverse.

MARYLAND: (See Philadelphia, PA), For Touch Screen Service, see reverse.

MASSACHUSETTS: Boston 🖳 Thos. P. O'Neill, Jr., Federal Bldg., 10 Causeway St., 02222, Staff on Duty: M-F/9-2, Self-Service: M-F/6-6, 24 Hour Telephone Service: (617) 565-5900

MICHIGAN: Detroit 🖳 477 Michigan Ave., Rm. 565, 48226, 24 Hour Telephone Service: (313) 226-6950, Staff on Duty: M-F/8-4:30

MINNESOTA: Twin Cities 🖳 Bishop Henry Whipple Federal Bldg., 1 Federal Dr., Rm. 501, Ft. Snelling, 55111, 24 Hour Telephone Service: (612) 725-3430, Staff on Duty: M-F/7:30-4:30, Self-Service: M-F/4:30-5:30

MISSISSIPPI: (See ALABAMA)

MISSOURI: Kansas City Federal Building, Rm. 134, 601 E. 12th St., 64106, 24 Hour Telephone Service: (816) 426-5702, Staff on Duty: M-F/8-4, (For Counties west of and including Mercer, Grundy, Carroll, Livingston, Saline, Pettis, Benton, Hickory, Dallas, Webster, Douglas, and Ozark)

St. Louis 🖳 400 Old Post Office Building, 815 Olive St., 63101, 24 Hour Telephone Service: (314) 539-2285, Self-Service: M-F/8-4, (For all other Missouri Counties not listed under Kansas City above)

MONTANA: (See COLORADO)

NEBRASKA: (See Kansas City, MO), 24 Hour Telephone Service: (816) 426-7819

NEVADA: (For Clark, Lincoln, and Nye Counties, see Los Angeles, CA), (For all other Nevada Counties not listed above, see Sacramento, CA)

NEW HAMPSHIRE: (See Boston, Massachusetts), For Touch Screen Service, see reverse.

NEW JERSEY: (For Bergen, Essex, Hudson, Hunterdon, Middlesex, Morris, Passaic, Somerset, Sussex, Union, and Warren Counties, see New York City, NY), (For Atlantic, Burlington, Camden, Cape May, Cumberland, Gloucester, Mercer, Monmouth, Ocean and Salem Counties, see Philadelphia, PA), For Touch Screen Service, see reverse.

NEW MEXICO: Albuquerque 🖳 505 Marquette Ave., Ste. 910, 87102, 24 Hour Telephone Service: (505) 766-5583, Staff on Duty: M-F/8-4

NEW YORK: New York City 🖳 Jacob K. Javits Federal Building, Second Floor, Rm. 120, 26 Federal Plaza, 10278, (212) 264-0422/0423, Staff on Duty: M-F/10-2, Self-Service: M-F/8-5

Syracuse P.O. Box 7257, 100 S. Clinton St., 13261, 24 Hour Telephone Service: (315) 448-0480, Self-Service: M-F/9-4

NORTH CAROLINA: Raleigh 🖳 4407 Bland Rd., Ste. 202, 27609, 24 Hour Telephone Service: (919) 790-2822, Staff on Duty: M-F/8-4:30

NORTH DAKOTA: (See MINNESOTA)

OHIO: Dayton Federal Building, Rm. 506, 200 W. 2nd St., 45402, 24 Hour Telephone Service: (513) 225-2720, Staff on Duty: M-F/8-4:45, (For Van Wert, Auglaize, Hardin, Marion, Crawford, Richland, Ashland, Wayne, Stark, Carroll, Columbiana Counties and farther north, see Michigan)

OKLAHOMA: (See San Antonio, TX)

OREGON: Portland 🖳 Federal Building, Rm. 376, 1220 SW. Third Ave., 97204, (503) 326-3141, Effective 02/14 — Self-Service only: M-F/8 12

PENNSYLVANIA: Harrisburg Federal Building, Rm. 168, P.O. Box 761, 17108, (717) 782-4494, Staff on Duty: MTThF/8-12

Philadelphia 🖳 Wm. J. Green, Jr., Federal Building, 600 Arch St., 19106, 24 Hour Telephone Service: (215) 597-7440, Staff on Duty: M-F/ 10:30-2:30, Self-Service: M-F/ 6:30-6:00

Pittsburgh Federal Building, 1000 Liberty Ave., Rm. 119, 15222, (Walk-in only. For mail or telephone, see Philadelphia listing), Self-Service: M-F/9-4

PUERTO RICO: San Juan 🖳 U.S. Federal Building, Rm. 328, 150 Carlos Chardon Ave., 00918, (809) 766-5242, Staff

on Duty: M-F/9-12:30, Self-Service: M-F/7:30-9; 12:30-4:00, 24 Hour Telephone Service: M-F Only at (809) 766-5242

RHODE ISLAND: (See Boston, Massachusetts), For Touch Screen Service, see reverse.

SOUTH CAROLINA: (See Raleigh, NC)

SOUTH DAKOTA: (See MINNESOTA)

TENNESSEE: (See ALABAMA), For Touch Screen Service, see reverse.

TEXAS: Corpus-Christi (See San Antonio) (512) 884-8113

Dallas (See San Antonio)

Harlingen (See San Antonio), (512) 412-0722

Houston (See San Antonio), (713) 759-0455

San Antonio 🖳 8610 Broadway, Rm. 305, 78217, (210) 805-2423, For forms call: (210) 805-2406, Staff on Duty: M-F/8-5, 24 Hour Telephone Service: (210) 805-2402

UTAH: (See COLORADO)

VERMONT: (See Boston, Massachusetts), For Touch Screen Service, see reverse.

VIRGIN ISLANDS: (See PUERTO RICO), (809) 774-8790

VIRGINIA: Norfolk 🖳 Touch Screen in Lobby. For mail only: Federal Building, Rm. 500, 200 Granby St., 23510, 24 Hour Telephone Service: (804) 441-3355, Telephone Service: M-F/8-4:00

For Walk-in only: National Guard Armory, 3777 E. Virginia Beach Blvd., Rm. 18A, OPM Staff on Duty: M-F/8:30-4:30

WASHINGTON: Seattle 🖳 Federal Building, Rm. 110, 915 Second Ave., 98174, 24 Hour Telephone Service: (206) 220-6400, Effective 02/14 — Self-Service only: M-F/8-12

WASHINGTON, DC: (See District of Columbia)

WEST VIRGINIA: (See OHIO), 24 Hour Telephone Service: (513) 225-2866

WISCONSIN: (For Dane, Grant, Green, Iowa, Lafayette, Jefferson, Walworth, Milwaukee, Racine, Waukesha, Rock, and Kenosha Counties, see Illinois listing), 24 Hour Telephone Service: (312) 353-6189, (For all other Counties not listed above, see Minnesota), 24 Hour Telephone Service: (612) 725-3430

WYOMING: (See COLORADO)

🖳 = Touch Screen Service Available

CE-22

Rev. 02-03-95

FRED GRIMES

4087 San Rafael Avenue
Los Angeles, CA 90065

January 30, 1996

George Zimmer, chairman
The Men's Wearhouse/Suits University
5803 Glenmont Drive
Houston, Texas 77081

Dear Mr. Zimmer:

I was watching t.v. the other day and I saw you lecturing at Suits University. All the students seemed real into it (not to mention real well dressed) and you seemed like you knew exactly what you were talking about. I especially like the part where you pointed your finger and said all confident like, "I guarantee it!"

Being unemployed I went down to the local Men's Wearhouse to see about getting a suit. I figure if I look my best on job interviews it might give me an advantage right? I realized that I could not afford a new suit right away but then I had an idea. Why not enroll in Suits University. I tried to ask some of the people at the Men's Wearhouse about SU but they all said they were pretty busy. They would not even tell me where it is!

I am writing to inquire about tuition, fees, room and board etc. etc. to Suits University. Would I have to live in the dorm? How many credits would I need to graduate. I already have one quarter in junior college. Would my credits transfer? What degrees are offered? Do you have financial aide? Are there athletic scholarships? Sir I do not mean to brag but I was the star of my softball team (references on request) before I lost my job down at the plant.

Mr. Zimmer, I just know I could do a good job at Suits University. "I guarantee it!"

Sincerely,

Fred Grimes
Fred Grimes

FRED GRIMES

2001 Grand Avenue
Santa Barbara, California 93103

August 16, 1996

Kenneth T. Derr, chairman and CEO
Chevron Oil Company
225 Bush Street
San Francisco, California 94104

Dear Mr. Derr:

How does somebody go about getting your company to put a oil well put on my property because I am wondering if there is oil under my back yard. I cannot say there is or there isnt. But you never know until you try right?

The well would have to be pretty small because my back yard is pretty small (references on request). Plus it would have to be pretty quiet because of the neighbors. My one neighbor works late and likes to sleep late on weekends. He gets to yelling if I crank up the leafblower too early. So you can imagine what would happen if oil started gushing! Does a gusher make a lot of noise? I know it makes a big mess. And how to you get all the spilled oil off the ground? Just curious.

Sir if you let me know I could make arrangements to put the dog inside so that your oil well experts could take a good look without being licked to death and figure out how far down they would have to go to hit pay dirt. Once the well is in you would not have to hire anybody to watch it because I am unemployed and pretty much do not go anywhere except for bowling once a week.

How much does something like this pay? Maybe we can go 50-50.

Sincerely,

Fred Grimes

Fred Grimes

September 16, 1996

Chevron U.S.A. Production Company
A Division of Chevron U.S.A. Inc.
P.O. Box 1392
Bakersfield, CA 93302
Fax 805 633 4545

Mr. Fred Grimes
2001 Grand Avenue
Santa Barbara, CA 93103

Dear Mr. Grimes:

Your letter to Mr. Ken Derr dated August 16, 1996 has, after passing through numerous hands, alighted on my desk for response.

While we sincerely enjoyed your letter and were indeed intrigued by your proposal, I must report that we have no interest in drilling in the area of your back yard and must therefore respectfully decline your kind offer.

Thank you for thinking of us and please go ahead and let the dog out.

Very truly yours,

DONN H. WILSON,
Division Land Manager

DHW/dm:F. Grimes Lease Offer.doc

FRED GRIMES

2001 Grand Avenue
Santa Barbara, California 93103

August 15, 1996

Gil Coronado, director
U.S. Selective Service System
National Headquarters
Arlington, Virginia 22209-2425

Dear Mr. Coronado:

Sir please do not take this the wrong way but what exactly does your office do these days?

The War has been over a long time. By the War I mean the Vietnam War which unless I am an idiot was the last time we had a draft. I know. Because I was there. I had to register for the draft and it was a scary thing let me tell you. But I was ready to do my duty to God and my Country. Had I not had a slight problem with the instep of my feet (references on request) I would have been over there kicking some serious Commie butt unlike a lot of guys I knew who had perfectly good feet and hightailed it for Canada!

Sir the reason I am writing you is to see if you might have any openings in your office. Not that I am lazy but if there is no more draft and not a lot going on any more with the Selective Service and you are still in business it would be the perfect place for me to work. I recently lost my job down at the plant and I do not have to tell you what kind of stress there is involved in being unemployed. The last thing I need is more stress!

Thanks for listening. I urgently await your reply.

Sincerely,

Fred Grimes

Fred Grimes

THE DIRECTOR OF SELECTIVE SERVICE
Arlington, Virginia 22209-2425

August 29, 1996

Mr. Fred Grimes
2001 Grand Avenue
Santa Barbara, California 93103

Dear Mr. Grimes:

Thank you for your letter of August 15, 1996. You are correct in noting that there has not been a draft since the Vietnam War, and we hope one will not be needed again. However, the Selective Service System is maintained in a standby, peacetime mode in case the United States should find itself in a crisis requiring more military manpower than is available in the standing Active and Reserve Forces. Since 1980, virtually all men turning 18 have been required to register with Selective Service in accordance with Federal law. If the President and the Congress determine that a draft is needed, the System is ready to supply manpower to the Armed Forces in a timely manner and to provide a program of alternative community service for men who are conscientious objectors.

President Clinton cited several reasons for maintaining Selective Service and the peacetime registration program. He noted it serves as a hedge against underestimating the forces America may face in a crisis, a symbol of national resolve to the Nation's potential adversaries, and a link between the all-volunteer military and American society-at-large. Currently, about 93 percent of all men 18 through 25 years old are registered. This high compliance rate, and maintenance of a low-cost System which includes 11,000 trained volunteer local board members, mean that any future draft will likely be the most fair and equitable draft in history.

If you are interested in applying for a job with the Selective Service System, or any Federal agency, I encourage you to contact the Office of Personnel Management at 202-606-2700, or write to OPM at 1900 E Street, N.W., Washington, D.C., 20415 to request an application for Federal employment. They can advise you of openings for which you may be qualified.

Sincerely,

Gil Coronado

FRED GRIMES

2001 Grand Avenue
Santa Barbara, California 93103

August 16, 1996

Herb Kelleher, president
Southwest Airlines
P.O. Box 36611
Love Field
Dallas, Texas 75235-1611

Dear Mr. Kelleher:

Do you need anybody to help fly your airplanes? If so count me in!

I do not actually know how to drive an airplane but I would be willing to learn. I should also tell you right up front that I get a little car sick when I fly. Is this a problem? The last time I got sick was in 1991 when I went to see my Uncle Ray and Aunt Jackie. It got a little bit bumpy over the Mountains. I do not have to tell you what happened next. I do not blame the pilot. And the stewardess who helped me to get cleaned up was real nice although I cannot say the same for the mean man who was sitting in the chair next to me. The view was great.

Sir I really like the new paint job on your airplanes. And the snacks. Penuts are my favorite. And _free_ soda! Do pilots get as much soda and penuts as they want. My friend Dave says they do. Talk about the good life! Plus they get to see a lot of very interesting places.

Driving a big airplane like a 747 looks pretty hard so I probably would want to start out on a smaller one right? What kinds of airplanes do you have? Please send my some photos so I can study them. I saw a story in the paper where some airplanes can take off and land all by themselves (references on request). Is this true? If so why do you even need somebody to drive?

I would be willing to fly just about anywhere except France.

Sincerely,

Fred Grimes

Fred Grimes

October 18, 1996

Mr. Fred Grimes
2001 Grand Avenue
Santa Barbara, CA 93103

Dear Mr. Grimes:

Thanks so much for your August 16 letter.

Although I was sorry to hear that you get "a little car sick" when you fly, I am glad to know that you enjoy the view. Incidentally, the view from the flight deck is awesome--you get to see many beautiful sunrises and sunsets.

I'm delighted that you enjoy our sodas and peanuts--they're my favorite too! Your friend, Dave, is right, our Pilots do eat and drink as many sodas and peanuts as they want.

Southwest Airlines only flies Boeing 737 aircraft, and it takes many years of training and flying to become a commercial Pilot. You may need to start out learning to fly something similar to a Cessna 152. I hope you will enjoy the photos of our aircraft and the "special" gift enclosed.

Thanks again for your kind comments, and we'll look forward to seeing you onboard one of our LUV jets in the near future!!

Best regards,

Herb Kelleher

Herbert D. Kelleher

HDK/lc

Copy to:
    Paul Sterbenz, Vice President Flight Operations
    Bill Miller, Vice President Inflight Services
    Joanne Lardon, Manager Provisioning Purchasing

P.S. The aviation industry is very exciting, and you would be amazed at what an aircraft is capable of doing on its own. Nonetheless, for overall safety, a Pilot "behind the wheel" is very important.

FRED GRIMES

2001 Grand Avenue
Santa Barbara, California 93103

August 16, 1996

Gordon Bethune, president
Continental Airlines
2929 Allen Parkway
Houston, Texas 77019

Dear Mr. Bethune:

Do you need anybody to help fly your airplanes? If so count me in!

I do not actually know how to drive an airplane but I would be willing to learn. I should also tell you right up front that I get a little car sick when I fly. Is this a problem? The last time I got sick was in 1991 when I went to see my Uncle Ray and Aunt Jackie. It got a little bit bumpy over the Mountains. I do not have to tell you what happened next. I do not blame the pilot. And the stewardess who helped me to get cleaned up was real nice although I cannot say the same for the mean man who was sitting in the chair next to me. The view was great.

Sir I really like the new paint job on your airplanes. And the snacks. Penuts are my favorite. And <u>free</u> soda! Do pilots get as much soda and penuts as they want. My friend Dave says they do. Talk about the good life! Plus they get to see a lot of very interesting places.

Driving a big airplane like a 747 looks pretty hard so I probably would want to start out on a smaller one right? What kinds of airplanes do you have? Please send my some photos so I can study them. I saw a story in the paper where some airplanes can take off and land all by themselves (references on request). Is this true? If so why do you even need somebody to drive?

I would be willing to fly just about anywhere except France.

Sincerely,

Fred Grimes

Fred Grimes

Continental

Continental Airlines, Inc.   Tel 713 987 6666
Suite 2010
2929 Allen Parkway
Houston TX 77019

August 22, 1996

Mr. Fred Grimes
2001 Grand Avenue
Santa Barbara, CA 93103

Dear Mr. Grimes:

Mr. Bethune received your letter and asked me to respond on his behalf. He asked me to thank you for your interest in Continental.

If you want to fly for us, you will need to take lots of lessons and fly the small planes for several thousand hours, then get a job for a commuter airline, then put in your application for the commuters with Continental Express. After flying the small planes, if you have the right degrees and background, you might get to be a Flight Engineer or Co-Pilot, then after several years more, you might become a Captain. Alternatively, some people join the Air Force and learn to be a pilot. In any case, it takes lots of years to "drive the big jets." You do get to eat all the peanuts you want.

Again, Mr. Grimes, thank you for your letter and your interest in Continental.

Sincerely,

Stella Young
Executive Assistant

FRED GRIMES

2001 Grand Avenue
Santa Barbara, California 93103

August 20, 1996

Donald D. Engen, director
National Air and Space Museum
6th and Independence Avenue S.W.
Washington, D.C. 20560

Dear Mr. Engen:

I always wanted to be an atronaut and blast off into outerspace. Maybe visit Mars. I wrote to NASA but it does not look like I have the "right stuff" as far as they are concerned. So I thought I would write you.

Mr. Engen I have a very exciting idea. How about hiring me to get dressed up like a real astronaut and talk to everybody that comes in to the museum. Sort of like an official greeter. I could stand by the door and pose for pictures with tourists and answer their questions about space travel etc. etc. I could maybe even be connected to a wire from the ceiling and show them what it is like to walk in space. Or jump down from the Luner Lander the way our brave boys did it on the Moon! "Thats one small step for man. One giant leap for mankind!" This way the real astronauts and other important people at the museum such as yourself could spend less time answering the same question 15 times and more time fixing up old airplanes and rocket ships etc. etc.

I have plenty of experience being on my feet all day (references on request) so you would not have to worry about me slacking off on the job. Sir it would be my honor to stand at the door of our greatest museum in an official U.S. Space Suit and welcome the citizens of this tiny blue marble we call planet earth.

Would I get my name on the Space Suit? That would be the best!

Sincerely,

Fred Grimes
Fred Grimes

NATIONAL AIR AND SPACE MUSEUM
SMITHSONIAN INSTITUTION
WASHINGTON. D.C. 20560

September 24, 1996

Mr. Fred Grimes
2001 Grand Avenue
Santa Barbara, California 93103

Dear Mr. Grimes:

Thank you for your kind letter of August 20 expressing your willingness to dress up like a real astronaut and greet visitors to the Smithsonian's National Air and Space Museum. Fortunately, the museum already has a dedicated group of volunteers and docents who greet our visitors, lead highlight tours of our galleries and provide other services along the lines you describe. Therefore, we must decline your gracious offer.

I wish you well and truly appreciate your interest in the Smithsonian's National Air and Space Museum.

Sincerely,

Michael Fetters
Office of Public Affairs

FRED GRIMES

ZZZZZZ

2001 Grand Avenue
Santa Barbara, California 93103

August 20, 1996

Dr. Michael S. Aldrich, director
Sleep Disorders Center
University of Michigan
1500 E. Medical Center Drive
Ann Arbor, Michigan 48107

Dear Dr. Aldrich:

I am wondering if you have any job openings to be a sleep research subject.

Sir I am an excellent sleeper (references on request). When my head hits that pillow I am out for a good 8 or 10 hours unless the cat wants to be fed at 3 in the morning at which time the Wife pushes me out of bed and makes me go down and feed him! Otherwise I am dead to the world so to speak. I can sleep through car alarms, dogs, earth quakes, the neighbors screaming and throwing things next door. You name it.

I would have no problem with you hooking up those electrical wires to my head and watching me or whatever it is you do to study these things. I want to contribute to science. By the way how much is the pay and is it by the hour. And do you get paid overtime for sleeping late. Just curious.

Doctor Aldrich I could start anytime.

Sincerely,

Fred Grimes

Fred Grimes

8 October 1996

Mr. Fred Grimes
2001 Grand Avenue
Santa Barbara, California   93103

Dear Mr. Grimes:

Thank you for your letter of September 16 concerning being a sleep research subject. At the moment, we do not have any protocols for which you would qualify but I will keep your name on file in case we begin any new protocols in the future for which you might be eligible.

Thank you for your interest.

Sincerely,

Michael S. Aldrich, M. D.
Associate Professor
Director, Sleep Disorders Center

MSA/dlb

FRED GRIMES

2001 Grand Avenue
Santa Barbara, California 93103

August 20, 1996

Bill Kurran, chairman
Nevada State Gaming Commission
1150 E. Williams Street
Carson City, Nevada 89710

Dear Mr. Kurran:

Before I lost my job down at the plant the Wife and I used to visit your fine state all the time to enjoy your many recreation activities. Not the least of which is slot machines.

I like the nickle slots myself. Your money goes a long way. You can sit there all night for $20. The Wife always went for the quarter slots. If I did not watch her she would go for the Silver Dollar slots (references on request). Talk about a high roller. You can lose a lot of money real quick playing Silver Dollar slot machines let me tell you!

Sir the reason I am writing is to see if you might hire me to go around Nevada and play the slot machines and make sure they are on the up and up. Here is my very exciting idea. The state would pay me to play the slots in Reno Vegas Taho etc. etc. You could stake me to what ever you think is fair. I personally think $5000 a month is fair. If I win I get to keep what ever I make. If I lose you are only out $5000. For your money I could report to you which casinos are paying off too much or not at all. I could also check out the 21 tables if you wanted. Or roulette. This could help the entire gambling industry I think don't you?

Mr. Kurran I am clean and trustworthy.

I anxiously await your reply.

Sincerely,

Fred Grimes
Fred Grimes

GOVERNOR BOB MILLER
Gaming Policy Committee Chairman

MARILYN EPLING, *Executive Secretary*

BILL CURRAN, *Chairman*
BOB J. LEWIS, *Member*
DEBORAH P. GRIFFIN, *Member*
WILLIAM R. URGA, *Member*
AUGIE GURROLA, *Member*

NEVADA GAMING COMMISSION

1150 E. William Street
Carson City, Nevada 89710
(702) 687-6530

August 27, 1996

Mr. Fred Grimes
2001 Grand Avenue
Santa Barbara, CA   93103

Dear Mr. Grimes:

This is in response to your letter to Chairman Bill Curran
proposing that the Nevada Gaming Commission hire you to gamble at
Nevada gaming establishments.

To provide background regarding gaming in Nevada I am enclosing a
copy of the publication "Gaming Nevada Style." As you will see,
the State Gaming Control Board is the body charged with the
responsibility of monitoring the activities of licensees and
ensuring that gaming is conducted in compliance with the laws and
regulations. That responsibility includes ongoing verifications
that slot machines are making appropriate payouts as well as
conducting dice and card inspections. As you see, the services
you proposed are performed by Board staff.

Thank you for your interest in Nevada's gaming industry, your
offer of assistance is appreciated.

Very truly yours,

Marilyn Epling
Executive Secretary

enc.

c: Bill Curran, Chairman

FRED GRIMES

2001 Grand Avenue
Santa Barbara, California 93103

August 20, 1996

Douglas Myers, director
San Diego Zoo
P.O. Box 551
San Diego, California 92112

Dear Mr. Myers:

I love animals. And I have a special way with them too (references on request). We have this cat. His name is Roy. I have taught him to do all kinds of amazing things like sit shake etc. etc. People are amazed when they come over to our house. The secret to training animals is to convince them that they <u>want</u> to do stuff instead of for the treat at the end am I right? And you have to pet them a lot.

Mr. Myers do you have an official petter? Somebody who goes around petting all our furry friends and giving them lots of love. If not I would like to put in for the job. I would pet all the animals. At least the ones who would not rip my arm off. I have always wanted to pet an elephant. What happens if they step on your foot? Good thing I already have boots so I could save you some money right there. Giraffes would be fun too but I would have to get on a ladder to scratch behind their ears and I am not real keen on heights!

I am not too crazy about snakes and bats either. They give me the creeps especially those real furry bats that hang upside down and make the squeeky noises. Talk about scary!

Sir I would be real careful with the bears. All these nuts on t.v. who are always climbing into the bear cages and then getting chewed on. What do you expect? You have to make friends with the bear first! They have to <u>trust</u> you.

Mr. Myers I could start any time.

Sincerely,

Fred Grimes
Fred Grimes

The Zoological Society of San Diego

September 13, 1996

Fred Grimes
2001 Grand Avenue
Santa Barbara, CA   93103

Dear Mr. Grimes:

Thank you for your offer to help with the animals in the San Diego Zoo; however, we use only our in-house keeper, health and research staff to care for them. For the most part, we avoid as much human interaction as possible with our exotic animals, because if they imprint on human beings, it can interfere with their natural behaviors and reproduction.

With your love of animals and gift of training them, you might consider volunteering to help your local humane society in working with abandoned domestic animals or there may be an organization in Santa Barbara that takes care of local wild animals in need of rehabilitation.

We appreciate your interest and taking the time to write.

Sincerely,

Douglas G. Myers
Executive Director

DGM/jbh

CELEBR80!
A World-Famous Birthday
1916 - 1996

Post Office Box 551, San Diego, California 92112-0551 USA Telephone (619) 231-1515 FAX (619) 231-0249

*Accredited by the American Zoo and Aquarium Association
and American Association of Museums*

FRED GRIMES

2001 Grand Avenue
Santa Barbara, California 93103

August 24, 1996

Steve Coz, editor
The National Enquirer
Lantana, Florida 33464

Dear Mr. Coz:

I would like to be a reporter for your newspaper.

The first big scoop I would write would be on Barbara Eden. Mr. Dolan I am a big fan of hers. I have seen every episode of I Dream Of Jeanie 100 times. Barbara Eden is the greatest actress in the world as far as I am concerned! I wrote her a letter but she did not reply. I wrote to her fan club and they did not rely. Maybe Barbara Eden isn't even alive any more. Or maybe she has been kidnapped. Enquiring minds like mine want to know!

Here is a poem I wrote for Barbara Eden:

Here's a story
Of a lovely Jeanie
Who lived in a bottle all alone
Until one day
When this one guy found her
And she lived hap-pi-ly.

I think it would be fun and rewarding to work for the Enquirer. I have never been a reporter before (references on request). How do you do it exactly? Get all the dirt I mean.

Mr. Coz just give me the word and I will get started on my Barbara Eden investigation.

Sincerely,

Fred Grimes

Fred Grimes

NATIONAL

ENQUIRER

LANTANA, FLORIDA 33464

(407) 586-1111

EXECUTIVE OFFICES

September 5, 1996

Mr. Fred Grimes
2001 Grand Avenue
Santa Barbara, CA 93103

Dear Mr. Grimes:

We are in receipt of your letter concerning a possible item for The National ENQUIRER, thank you, we appreciate your interest.

We are sure you will appreciate that we receive a vast number of suggestions and are able to publish only a small number of them and I regret that yours is one of those our editors have decided they are unable to use.

The publisher assumes no responsibility for returning unsolicited manuscripts, photographs, art work, letters or other like material.

Thanks again for thinking of us, we hope you will continue to enjoy reading The National ENQUIRER.

As to your interest in reporting for The National ENQUIRER I'm sorry to say that at present we are not hiring intern reporters.

Sincerely yours,

Rose W. Clark
Sr. Editorial Assistant
to Executive Editor Steve Coz

SWC/rwc

FRED GRIMES

2001 Grand Avenue
Santa Barbara, California 93103

September 4, 1996

James van Loben Sels, director
California Department of Transportation
P.O. Box 942873
Sacramento, California 94273

Dear Mr. van Loben Sels:

I applied for a job to Mr. Rodney E. Slater of the Federal Highway Department. I told him I wanted to go around the Country and check on the highways for him and stay at the Ramada etc. etc. Anyway he turned me down and said I should write to you for work.

Mr. van Loben Sels it is a good thing Mr. Slater said no because it got me to thinking and I have a _real_ exciting idea for you. Sir do you remember a show on t.v. about a couple of fellows in a Corvette Stingray who drive up and down route 66 meeting girls and having adventures etc. etc.? I cannot remember the name of the show but it was very exciting (references on request). Sir how about me doing the same thing?

Mr. van Loben Sels think about it. If the state of California was to buy me a Corvette Stingray and pay me to drive up and down route 66 I could not only tell you what the road conditions was like so you could make repairs but I could also get a _ton_ of publicity. Think of all the tourists who would come to California and spend all their money. Billions. I could have all sorts of adventures and help Our Great State too!

If the state of California does not want to spring for a Corvette I guess I could always drive the Wifes car. If she would let me. It is a Saturn. Saturns are nice cars but they are no Corvette Stingray I am here to tell you which is probably a good thing in my case when I think about it because you are a lot more likely to have "adventures" in a Stingray and wind up in divorce court if you get my drift and I think you do.

Mr. van Loben Sels I promise I would not speed or be a menace on the road.

Sincerely,

Fred Grimes

Fred Grimes

DEPARTMENT OF TRANSPORTATION
OFFICE OF THE DIRECTOR
1120 N STREET
P. O. BOX 942873
SACRAMENTO, CA 94273-0001
PHONE (916) 654-5782
FAX (916) 654-6608

September 19, 1996

Mr. Fred Grimes
2001 Grand Avenue
Santa Barbara, CA 93103

Dear Mr. Grimes:

Caltrans Director James van Loben Sels asked me to respond to your letter.

Your idea about driving Route 66 in a Corvette Stingray is probably a dream shared by most of us from the generation that remembers the exploits of Martin Milner and George Maharis from that television program "Route 66."

Unfortunately, Caltrans is not in the position of granting your request. First, Route 66 is no longer a state highway, replaced by Interstate 40 which opened in the 1960s. To direct precious state transportation resources to "promoting" Route 66 would be an inappropriate use of state gas tax money paid by motorists. The mission of the California Department of Transportation is to build, operate and maintain the state transportation system.

Finally, there are organizations like the Route 66 Association and the California Office of Tourism that are responsible for promoting interest in Route 66 and other landmarks in California.

Good luck in your efforts. And if you find someone willing to pay you to cruise around in a 'Vette, please let me know.

Sincerely,

MICHAEL BRENNAN
Deputy Director
External Affairs

FRED GRIMES

2001 Grand Avenue
Santa Barbara, California 93103

August 26, 1996

Ambassador Francois Bujon De L'estang
4101 Reservoir Road
Washington, D.C. 20007

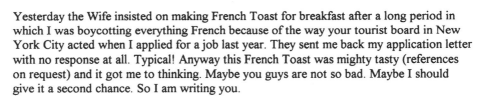

Dear Mr. Ambassador:

Bonjour.

Yesterday the Wife insisted on making French Toast for breakfast after a long period in which I was boycotting everything French because of the way your tourist board in New York City acted when I applied for a job last year. They sent me back my application letter with no response at all. Typical! Anyway this French Toast was mighty tasty (references on request) and it got me to thinking. Maybe you guys are not so bad. Maybe I should give it a second chance. So I am writing you.

Mr. Ambassador I was thinking that maybe you should hire me an ordinary American to go around France and help teach your country men what ordinary Americans really like and are like. This way more of us would feel comfortable going over to France and spending our hard earned green backs (dollars) to help you guys out!

Sir with all due respect lesson number one is improving your attitude. Like when I called your office today to get your address. Your receptionist was not exactly what we Americans would call friendly. I had a dog of a time just trying to understanding her. When I asked her to please spell out your name for me she kept saying "la upholstery" and got more and more snooty when I made her repeat the "la upholstery" part until I finally figured out what she was trying to say--"a postraphe." Mr. Ambassador I do not mind telling you that she made me feel like an idiot! Sir most Americans do not have a postraphe in their names. How was I supposed to know what she was talking about?

Sincerely,

Fred Grimes

Fred Grimes

FRED GRIMES

2001 Grand Avenue
Santa Barbara, California 93103

Mayor Rudolph Giuliani
City of New York
City Hall
New York, New York 10007

Dear Mr. Mayor:

Maybe this does not come as a surprise to you but a lot of people out here in California say a lot of bad things about New York City. Crowds. Muggers. The weather. New Yorkers etc. etc.

Mr. Mayor I think this is not fair to your fair city. I have never been to the Big Apple but how bad can it be? If it is so bad why do so many people live there? Big important people. Such as yourself. When I tell this to my friends they look at me like I am a few beers short of a six pack. My friend Dave says, "You couldn't pay me enough to live in New York." Well you could me.

Mr. Mayor how about paying me to live in New York? Call it a temporary job. You could put the Wife and me up in a nice hotel and pick up our meals for $5,000 a month easy. We could go to the movies or watch the Today Show or go hang out in Central Park. Then we could come back home and tell everybody how great New York City is. I bet a lot of people would go visit New York City after that. They would come home and tell their friends what a good time they had. Their friends would go to New York City and tell their friends. Their friends would tell their friends etc. etc. Think of the money everybody in New York City would make off all these visitors. Billions I bet!

Sir I have not approached any other Mayors like Cleveland or Newark with this exciting idea because I wanted to give New York City first crack. As I am currently without work I could be ready to go out there any time. Just let me know.

Sincerely,

Fred Grimes

Fred Grimes

FRED GRIMES

2001 Grand Avenue
Santa Barbara, California 93103

September 16, 1996

Mayor Rudolph Giuliani
New York City
City Hall
New York, New York 10007

Dear Mr. Mayor:

I wrote to you almost a month ago about being a sort of West Coast ambassador to your fair city. I have not heard from you.

Sir I am sure that you are a busy person running New York City but what gives? I am a big supporter of the Big Apple. I would think the least I deserve is an answer one way or the other.

Thank you!

Sincerely,

Fred Grimes

Fred Grimes

September 27, 1996

Mr. Fred Grimes
2001 Grand Avenue
Santa Barbara, California 93103

Dear Mr. Grimes:

I write on behalf of Mayor Giuliani in response to your recent letter. Thank you for writing and sharing your views on New York City, "The Capital of the World." This administration has made significant changes in the quality of life in New York City. There has been a considerable rise in tourism, and crime rates have been reduced significantly. Please be assured that we are working hard to make New York City a better place to live.

Thank you for writing the Office of the Mayor.

Sincerely,

Bruce Teitelbaum
Acting Chief of Staff

BT:mz

FRED GRIMES

2001 Grand Avenue
Santa Barbara, California 93103

October 4, 1996

Bruce Teitelbaum, acting chief of staff
Office of Mayor Rudolph Giuliani
City of New York
City Hall
New York, New York 10007

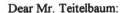

NO REPLY

Dear Mr. Teitelbaum:

Did you even read my letter?

I wrote to Mayor Giuliani about wanting a job as a kind of West Coast goodwill ambassador for New York City. I was not "sharing my views" on New York City. All I was saying was that a lot of people out here think you folks back there live in a smelly dangerous rat infested dump, a place where men are men and the women are men.

Of course that is not to say I believe these things. I am just telling you what people are saying.

Sir I think it is great that there has been a "considerable rise in tourism and crime rates have been reduced significantly" in New York City thanks to your hard work. But this does not answer the question I asked in the first place which is can I have a job yes or no?

Sincerely,

Fred Grimes

Fred Grimes

P.S.--Maybe if you got some better sports teams...

FRED GRIMES

2001 Grand Avenue
Santa Barbara, California 93103

November 8, 1996

Mr. John Sargent, chairman and CEO
St. Martin's Press
175 Fifth Avenue
New York, New York 10010

Dear Sgt:

Boy do I love books. You name it. Car repair books. Books about baseball. Books with Cindy Crawford. You give me a good book and I will read it! (references on request).

Sir let me get right to the point. I am unemployed. I worked down at the plant. Then I lost my job. It got me to thinking. What would be the perfect job? Then it hit me like a bolt of thunder. Fred, if you like to read books so much why not sell them? Combine business with pleasure. This is why I am writing you. To be a sales representative for your fine company.

I can only imagine the excitement and satisfaction of going all over the place and selling books. Having conversations about books. Staying in hotels, eating on the company dime etc. etc. . Talk about the good life! The only problem as I see is having to lug all those books all over the place. Dragging them out of the car and into the store. I hurt my back down at the plant so I cannot do heavy lifting even with one of those special belts everybody is wearing now. Maybe you can hire me an assistant to lug all the books around. Good thing you do not sell Encyclopedia Britanica! You don't, do you?

Mr. Sargent, I could start any time.

Sincerely,

Fred Grimes

Fred Grimes

P.S. Were you ever in the Army? It must have been pretty weird if so. Did they call you Private Sergeant when you were at boot camp? Talk about confusing!

ST. MARTIN'S PRESS

John Sargent
Chief Executive Officer

November 12, 1996

Mr. Fred Grimes
2001 Grand Avenue
Santa Barbara, California 93103

Dear Mr. Grimes,

Thanks for your letter. We don't sell Encyclopedia Britanica (which is a good thing), I was never in the army or boot camp (which is a good thing) and we don't have any open sales territories.

Good luck in your search.

Best,